The Complete Photo Guide to
Slipcovers

The Complete Photo Guide to
Slipcovers

Transform Your Furniture with Classic or Casual Covers

EDITED BY LINDA NEUBAUER

Creative Publishing international

Chanhassen, MN

Creative Publishing
international

Copyright 2007
Creative Publishing international
18705 Lake Drive East
Chanhassen, Minnesota 55317
1-800-328-3895
www.creativepub.com
All rights reserved

President/CEO: Ken Fund
Executive Editor: Alison Brown Cerier
Executive Managing Editor: Barbara Harold
Senior Editor: Linda Neubauer
Photo Stylist: Joanne Wawra
Creative Director: Brad Springer
Photographers: Peter Caley and Andrea Rugg
Production Manager: Linda Halls
Cover Design: Brian Donahue/bedesign, inc.
Page Design and Layout: Brian Donahue/bedesign, inc.

Library of Congress Cataloging-in-Publication Data

The Complete photo guide to slipcovers : transform your furniture
with fitted or casual covers / edited by Linda Neubauer.
    p. cm.
 ISBN-13: 978-1-58923-271-6 (soft cover)
 ISBN-10: 1-58923-271-2 (soft cover)
 1. Slip covers. I. Neubauer, Linda. II. Title.
 TT395.C66 2007
 746.9'5--dc22   2006021438

Printed in China
10 9 8 7 6 5 4 3 2 1

Contents

Furniture Facelifts

You don't have to buy new furniture to give your home a new look. In fact, you may love your furniture's style and the way if fits you, though you've grown a little tired of the color or pattern. Slipcovers can give your furniture a fresh start when you want to change the color scheme of a room, update faded or worn upholstery, or simply alter the mood with the changing of the seasons.

Slipcovers can also modify the style of your furnishings a bit. You are limited somewhat by your furniture's original lines—a wing chair will always be a wing chair—but you can make a slipcover that will change the look considerably. For instance, a stately Edwardian wing chair, upholstered in an elegant jacquard fabric, works great in a traditional living room. However, given a floral cotton slipcover with a short ruffled skirt, that same chair takes on a cheerful, romantic appearance more suitable for a country bedroom. Unmatched pieces you've acquired at sales or secondhand shops can be slipcovered in matching or coordinating fabrics to unify them.

If your favorite chair still has firm padding and a sturdy frame, a fitted slipcover is a great alternative to reupholstery. Hugging the chair like a glove, a fitted slipcover gives the chair new life without changing its identity, and with far less commitment than stripping the original cover and reupholstering. With slipcovers, family heirlooms and cherished antiques can retain their valuable "first skins" while playing an active role in your decorating plan.

The projects in this book are typical furniture candidates for slipcovers. With variations in fabrics, skirt styles, and closures, you can mix and match techniques to design slipcovers that are just right for your furniture and décor. For many of the projects, the instructions first take you step-by-step through pin-fitting a *muslin* pattern onto the furniture. Experienced slipcover makers often do the pin-fitting with the decorator fabric, which saves time but can also be costly if a mistake is made. Another benefit of making a muslin pattern is that you can keep the pattern to make additional slipcovers for the same piece of furniture. Some slipcovers are easy enough to make simply by measuring the furniture and cutting rectangles of fabric. Separate cutting instructions are given for many of the projects. For some slipcovers, the cutting directions are incorporated into the instructions.

Each project includes a materials list of everything you'll probably have to buy. The list doesn't tell you how much fabric to buy because that depends on the size of your furniture and the size of the pattern repeat for printed fabrics. The list also assumes you have on hand basic sewing supplies, such as pins, fabric shears, tape measure, fabric marking pens or pencils, sewing machine and attachments, thread, iron, and pressing surface. Also included with each project are cutting directions and some advice to help you choose fabric and slipcover details for that particular furniture piece. Step-by-step instructions are accompanied by photographs to help you make slipcovers you'll be proud to show off in your home. Check out the Terms to Know on page 112 if you come across unfamiliar words and phrases.

Choosing the Right Fabric

To help you choose fabrics for your slipcovers, consider what effect you want the furniture to have in the room. While color and design play an important part in the decision, it is also important to consider the fiber content, weave structure, and any surface treatment applied to the fabric.

You should make your slipcovers with decorator fabrics. These differ from fashion fabrics in several ways. Decorator fabrics are generally more durable than fashion fabrics. Often they are treated with a stain-resistant or crease-resistant finish. For this reason, most decorator fabrics must be dry cleaned rather than laundered—especially important for slipcovers because shrinkage can be disastrous. Unlike fashion fabrics, decorator fabrics with designs are printed or woven to match from one *selvage* to the next, so that any necessary seams in large pieces are less visible. The fabric identification label gives the measurement of the pattern repeats. The vertical repeat is the distance up and down between points where the pattern repeats itself. The horizontal repeat is often given also, especially for larger prints. This information is necessary

for determining the amount of fabric needed for a slipcover. Large motifs in a pattern must be centered on cushion tops and bottoms, chair backs, and arms. Ideally, a pattern should flow uninterrupted from the top to the bottom of the slipcover.

The scale of a print is also an important consideration. Large prints may overpower a small chair slipcover, just as tiny all-over prints can get lost on a large sofa slipcover.

If you want to use several prints in the same room, select coordinating prints in various sizes, and add solid color accents.

Fabrics can be grouped into categories according to their weave or surface design. Plain weaves (1) are the simplest of weaves. They may be solid in color or printed, and their strength is determined by the closeness of the yarns in the weave. Satin weaves (2) are woven so that yarns float on the surface, giv-

Performance fabrics intended for use outdoors look and feel like interior decorator fabrics and are available in some of the same prints and colors.

ing the fabric a subtle sheen. They also may be solid in color or printed. Jacquard weaves (3), including damasks, tapestries, and brocades, have woven-in designs. Novelty weaves (4), often single colors, feature textural interest created by complicated weave patterns. These fabrics are very versatile in any color scheme. Pile fabrics (5), such as suede, corduroy, and chenille, have interesting surface textures.

Decorator fabrics for the interior are often made of natural fibers, which include cotton, linen, silk, and wool. Natural fibers are breathable, comfortable, and easy to sew. Unfortunately, these fabrics don't perform very well for porches, sunrooms, or outdoors. To keep up with the strong trend toward outdoor decorating, manufacturers are also making water-repellant, fade-resistant, acrylic or polyester decorator fabrics that look and feel like interior fabrics. They are colorfast and are treated to resist stains and mildew.

Reversible Seat Cover

● ● ○

Simple seat covers give your dining room or kitchen chairs a fresh look. These covers are made with two coordinating decorator fabrics, so they can be flipped over for an instant décor change. Darts sewn at the front corners shape the covers to fit the chair seats smoothly. The back corners are held in place with a button tab that wraps around the back of the leg.

What you'll need

- (+) Muslin for making patterns

- (+) Two coordinating decorator fabrics, such as a print and a stripe; amount depends on chair size and fabric design size

- (+) Four buttons for each cover, $7/8"$ to 1" (2.2 to 2.5 cm) in diameter

- (+) $1/2$ yd. (0.5 m) grosgrain ribbon, $7/8"$ (2.2 cm) wide, in a color to match the fabrics

What you need to know

These covers wrap over all four edges of the seat, so they are suitable for armless chairs with straight sides and fronts that are open between the back posts. Because the amount of fabric needed depends on your chair size and the fabric design size, make the pattern first so you'll know how much fabric to buy.

When making covers for two or more chairs, you'll want to center the same motif on each seat cover. If you choose fabric with large motifs, such as the toile used on page 10, take the pattern with you when you shop for fabric.

Seat covers

1. Measure the chair seat side to side and front to back. Add 10" (25.5 cm) in each direction. Cut muslin to this size to make a pattern. Press the muslin pattern in half in both directions. Unfold. Center the pattern on the chair seat, allowing it to fall down over the front and sides. At the back, turn the pattern up along the posts. If necessary, tape the pattern in place.

2. Mark a dot at one front corner. Pinch the fabric together from the dot down, bringing the front to meet the side. Pin out excess fabric, inserting the pins parallel to the chair leg, forming a dart. Mark lines on both sides of the dart from the dot down to the bottom. Repeat on the other front corner.

3. Mark dots at the back of the seat, at the inside front corners of the back posts. (If your posts are round, mark each dot at a point in line with the front and side of the post.) Trace the outline of the chair seat on the pattern.

4. Remove the pattern from the chair; remove the pins. Draw lines $4^{1}/2"$ (11.5 cm) outside the traced seat lines. At the back corners, draw lines from the dots to the outer lines, forming squares. (These will be the stitching lines.) Mark pivot points (shown in blue) on the stitching lines $1/2"$ (1.3 cm) from the outer edge. Draw cutting lines (shown in red) $1/2"$ (1.3 cm) outside the stitching lines at the legs and the front darts. Fold the pattern in half to make sure it is symmetrical, and make any necessary corrections. Cut out the pattern on the outer lines.

5. Place the pattern on the top fabric, aligning the front-to-back crease with the lengthwise grain and the side-to-side crease with the crosswise grain. Position the pattern so that the intersection of the creases is at the exact center of the design motif, if using a large print. Cut out the seat cover top. Transfer the pivot points and dart dots to the wrong side of the fabric.

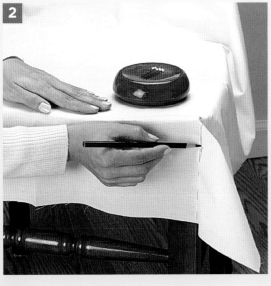

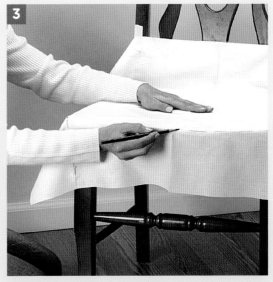

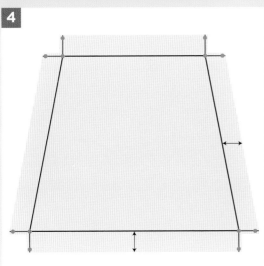

6. Cut out the remaining seat cover tops, using the first piece as a guide. This will make it easier to center the design motifs. Place each of the tops on the bottom fabric, right sides together. Pin near the outer edges. Cut them out; remove the pins.

7. Fold the dart on one front corner, right sides together, aligning the raw edges; pin. Stitch the dart.

8. Repeat step 7 for the remaining front corners on the top and bottom pieces. Press the seam allowances of the darts open.

Continued >>

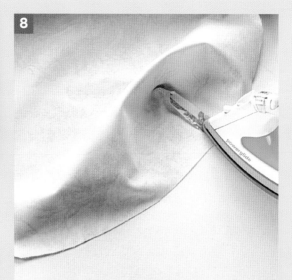

9. Place the top and bottom seat covers right sides together, aligning the raw edges; pin. Align the seams of the front darts. Stitch the layers together ½" (1.3 cm) from the edge all around, pivoting at the corners. Leave a 6" (15 cm) opening along one straight edge for turning.

10. Trim the seam allowances diagonally at the outer corners. Clip to, but not through, the stitches at the inner corners.

11. Turn back the top seam allowances and press, applying light pressure with the tip of the iron down the crease of the seam. In the area of the opening, turn back and press the seam allowances ½" (1.3 cm) where they meet.

12. Turn the cover right side out through the opening. Insert a point turner or similar tool into the opening and gently push the pivot points out to form perfect corners. Push the seam out so that it is centered all around the outer edge; press. Align the folded edges of the opening and pin them closed.

13. Edgestitch around the seat cover, stitching the opening closed; pivot at the corners.

14. Mark placement lines for the four button-holes parallel to and 1" (2.5 cm) above the lower side and back edges. Mark lines that equal the diameter plus the thickness of the buttons, with one end 1" (2.5 cm) from the vertical edges. Attach a buttonhole presser foot or buttonhole attachment. Stitch the buttonholes over the marked lines. Cut the buttonholes open, using a buttonhole cutter or small, sharp scissors.

15. Place the cover on the chair seat. At the back of one chair leg, measure the distance between buttonholes. Cut ribbon 4" (10 cm) longer than this measurement. Turn under 1" (2.5 cm) twice on each end of the ribbon; press. Stitch across the inner folds, forming double-fold hems. Stitch a button to the center of each hem. Repeat for the other leg. Button the chair seat cover in place.

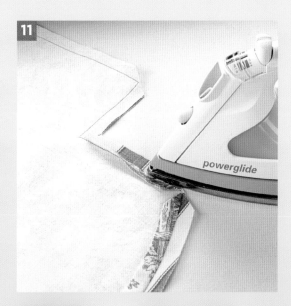

Tip

Pressing seam allowances open before turning a lined piece right side out makes the seam lay smoothly along the edge. Often this means pressing the upper layer back as in step 10.

Kitchen and Dining Chairs

● ● ○

Two-piece slipcovers can be used on simple kitchen or dining room chairs to update a look or help soften the room with fabric. Slipcovers are also a great way to cover up worn or unmatched chairs. This slipcover style can range from shabby chic to tailored and formal, depending on the fabric choice and detailing of the cover.

What you'll need

- Muslin for making patterns
- Decorator fabric
- Lining
- Fabric for welting
- Cording for welting
- Twill tape, 1" (2.5 cm) wide

What you need to know

Both pieces of this slipcover are lined for durability and body. Welting, applied around the seat slipcover and along the lower edge of the back slipcover, defines and supports the edges.

These covers wrap over all four edges of the seat, so they are suitable for armless chairs that are open between the back posts and have straight sides and fronts. Decorative ties are secured to the back posts; concealed twill-tape ties secure the cover to the front legs of the chair.

The back slipcover and the skirt on the chair seat can be any length you want. For back slipcovers that are long, the back of the chair must be straight to the upper edge or taper only slightly inward; if the top of the chair back is wider than the bottom, it will not be possible to slip the cover on. To help you decide on the best length for your project, take into account the style and detailing of the chair. For a nice drape and an attractive appearance, make the skirt at least 5" to 6" (12.7 to 15 cm) long and end the skirt slightly above or below any cross pieces of the chair. The seat slipcover can be made with either clustered gathers, as shown on page 17, or pleats at the front corners, like the Parsons chair (page 24) and the ottoman (page 31).

Cutting directions

- Make the seat and back patterns as on pages 19 and 20. Cut one seat each from the decorator fabric and the lining; transfer the marks. Cut one front and one back from both the decorator fabric and the lining; transfer the marks.

- For a gathered skirt, cut the fabric as on pages 20 and steps 1 and 2.

- Cut 1⅝" (4 cm) bias strips for welting. The combined length of the strips is equal to the circumference of the seat cover and the lower edge of the back cover; allow extra for seams and overlaps.

- Cut eight fabric strips 1½" (3.8 cm) wide and 10" to 16" (25.5 to 40.5 cm) long for the back ties on the seat cover. Cut four 12" (30.5 cm) lengths of twill tape for the concealed front ties.

Chair seat slipcover pattern

1. Measure the chair seat side to side and front to back. Add 6" (15 cm) in each direction. Cut muslin to size. Mark the center line on the lengthwise grain. Center the muslin on the seat; pin or tape in place. Using a pencil, mark the outer rim of the seat front, and sides to back posts, rounding square corners slightly. Mark the placement for front ties.

2. Mark the back edge of the chair seat on the muslin; clip the fabric as necessary for a snug fit if the seat is shaped around back posts. Mark the placement of the skirt back between the chair posts.

3. Remove the pattern from the chair. Redraw seam lines as necessary, using a straight-edge; redraw curved lines, drawing smooth curves. Reposition the pattern on the chair to check the fit; adjust as necessary.

4. Add ½" (1.3 cm) seam allowances to the pattern and cut it out.

Chair back slipcover pattern—straight upper edge

1. Measure the chair back; cut two pieces of muslin about 6" (15 cm) wider and 2" (5 cm) longer than the measurements. Mark a line 1" (2.5 cm) from the edge for the chair back; pin the pieces together on the marked line. Center the muslin on the chair with the marked line at the upper edge.

2. Pin the muslin at the sides of the chair, allowing ample ease. Mark the desired finished length. Pull gently on the cover to make sure it slides off easily; adjust the width or length of the cover, if necessary.

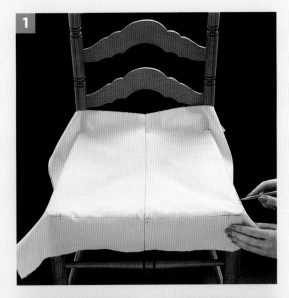

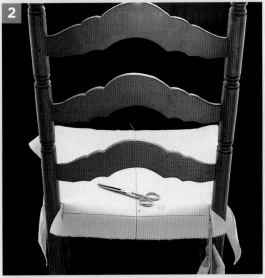

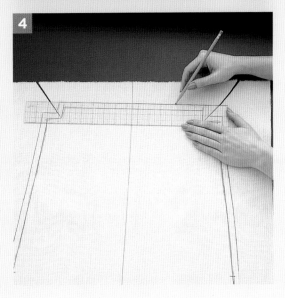

Continued >>

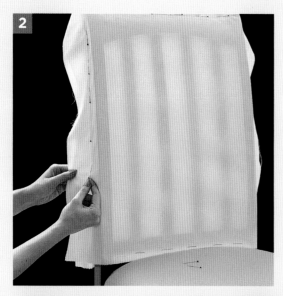

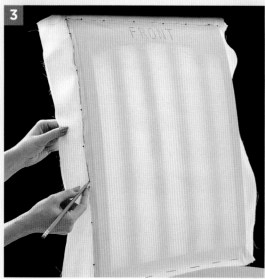

3. Mark the seam lines, following pin placement. Label the patterns for front and back.

4. Remove the muslin from the chair. Redraw the seam lines if necessary, using a straight-edge. Repin the muslin, and position on the chairs; adjust as necessary. The front and back of the pattern may be different sizes.

5. Mark ½" (1.3 cm) seam allowances; mark the grain line. Cut out the pattern.

Shaped upper edge

1. Measure the chair back; cut two pieces of muslin about 6" (15 cm) larger than these measurements. Pin pieces together at the upper edge, and center over the chair back; adjust pins to follow contours of the chair, simplifying design as necessary. Continue as for chair back with straight upper edge, steps 2 to 4; in step 4, smooth any curved lines. Complete the pattern as in step 5.

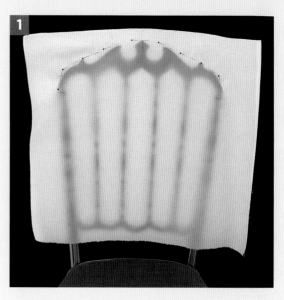

Sewing the chair seat slipcover

1. Measure the pattern seam line around the front and sides of the seat between markings at the back posts; add 12" (30.5 cm) for the corner gathers plus 1" (2.5 cm) for seam allowances. Cut the fabric strip for the front skirt to this length, piecing fabric, if necessary; the width of the strip is equal to twice the desired finished skirt length plus 1" (2.5 cm) for seam allowances.

2. Measure the pattern seam line between markings for the back skirt. Cut the fabric strip for the back skirt to this length plus 1" (2.5 cm); the width of the strip is equal to twice the desired finished skirt length plus 1" (2.5 cm) for seam allowances.

3. Staystitch any inner corners and curves on the chair seat top and lining. Clip to, but not through, the stitching as necessary.

4. Make welting, if desired, and apply to the seat top as on page 110. Place two tie strips right sides together; stitch ¼" (6 mm) seam on the long sides and one short end of the tie. Trim corners and turn right side out; press. Pin the ties to the right side of the seat top at the back corners, aligning the raw edges.

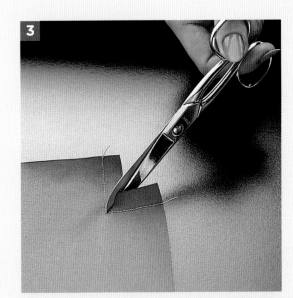

5. Fold the skirt front in half lengthwise, right sides together; stitch ½" (1.3 cm) seams on the short ends. Turn right side out; press. Repeat for the skirt back.

6. Pin-mark the center of the skirt at the raw edges. Measure the edge of the seat pattern on the seam line, from center front to corner; add 3" (7.5 cm). Measure this distance out from the center of the skirt, and pin-mark for corners. Clip-mark the skirt 6" (15 cm) from both sides of the corner pin marks.

7. Stitch two rows of gathering threads along the upper edge of the skirt front between the clip marks, ¼" (6 mm) and ½" (1.3 cm) from the raw edges.

8. Pin the skirt front to the seat top, right sides together, matching the raw edges and markings for center front and corners. Pull the gathering threads to fit. Machine-baste the skirt to the seat top, using a zipper foot.

9. Pin the skirt back to the seat top, right sides together, matching the raw edges; stitch.

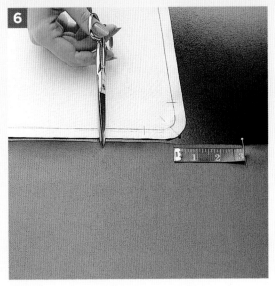

10. Pin or baste twill-tape ties to the wrong side of the skirt at front-corner marks.

11. Pin the skirt and ties to the seat to prevent catching them in the seams. Pin the lining to the seat, with right sides together and raw edges even. Stitch, leaving a 6" (15 cm) center opening in the back. Trim seam allowance; clip the curves and corners.

Continued >>

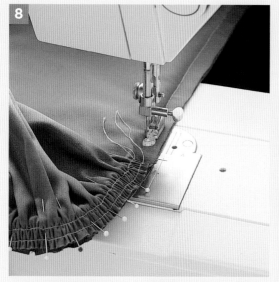

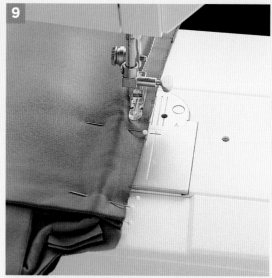

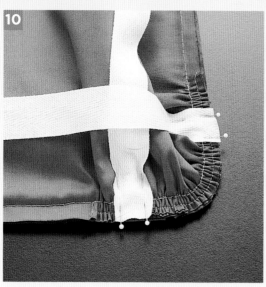

12. Turn the seat cover right side out; press. Slipstitch the opening closed. Position the seat cover on the chair; secure the back ties in a bow or square knot. Lift the skirt, and secure the front ties; trim any excess length.

Sewing the chair back slipcover—straight upper edge

1. Place the front and the back decorator fabric pieces right sides together, matching the raw edges. Stitch ½" (1.3 cm) seam around the sides and upper edge. Press the seam open.

2. To accommodate the thickness of the chair back, open the corners, aligning the seam allowances; stitch across the corners a distance equal to the thickness of the chair back. Trim the seam.

3. Attach the welting, if desired, to the lower edge of the outer cover as on page 111, steps 2 to 5. Stitch the lining as for the outer cover, leaving a 6" (15 cm) center opening on one side. Press the seam allowances open.

4. Place the decorator fabric and lining right sides together, matching the lower edge; stitch ½" (1.3 cm) seam.

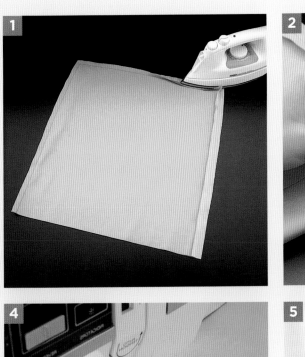

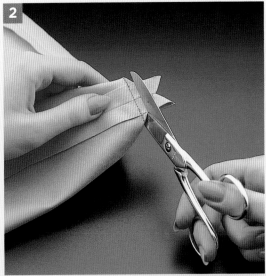

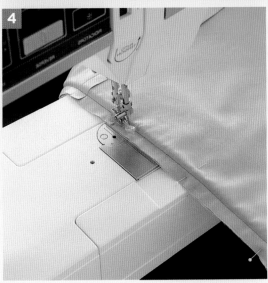

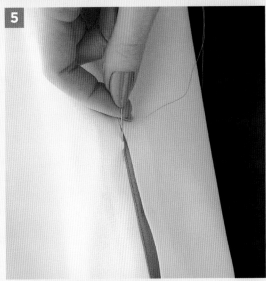

5. Turn the slipcover, lining side out, through the opening in the lining; press the lower edge. Slipstitch the opening closed. Turn the slipcover right side out; place over the back of the chair.

Shaped upper edge

1. Place the front and back decorator fabric pieces right sides together, matching the raw edges. Stitch ½" (1.3 cm) seam around the sides and upper edge; press open. Trim the seam; clip any curves. Complete as in steps 3 to 5 for straight upper edge.

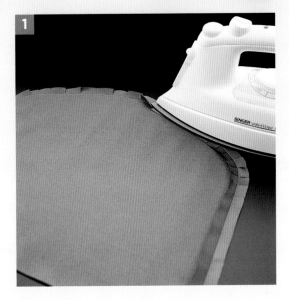

Parsons Chairs

● ● ●

Parsons chairs are popular dining room chairs, with upholstered backs that adjoin upholstered seats. The lines are very tailored and straight, and there is often a floor-length skirt. These one-piece slipcovers conceal the entire chair and have skirts with inverted box pleats at the corners.

What you'll need

- ☐ Muslin for pattern
- ☐ Decorator fabric
- ☐ Contrasting fabric for welting, optional
- ☐ Cording for welting, optional

What you need to know

These covers are suitable for chairs with straight backs. The upper edge of the chair back must be no wider than the lower back, or you won't be able to slip the cover on. When measuring the front and back of the chair back, measure as if there are centered side seams, even if the seams on the upholstered chair are not centered.

The skirt for this style is self-lined, eliminating any noticeable hemline and giving the skirt extra body.

Pin-fitting the pattern

1. Measure the length and width of the front of the chair back. Add 4" (10 cm) to the length and the width. Cut muslin to size. Mark a center line on the lengthwise grain. Mark a line 1" (2.5 cm) from the raw edge at the upper edge on the muslin.

2. Repeat step 1 for the back of the chair back. Label the pattern pieces.

3. Pin the front and back pattern pieces of the chair back, wrong sides together, at the upper marked line matching the center lines. Center the patterns on the chair back and pin the patterns at the sides of the chair, allowing ample ease. Mark the side seams on both the front and back pieces.

4. Measure the length of the chair seat from the back to where the cushion meets the frame at the front. Measure the width from where the cushion meets the frame at the sides. Cut muslin 6" (15 cm) larger than measurement. Mark a center line on the lengthwise grain. Label the pattern piece.

5. Press under 1" (2.5 cm) along the back of the chair seat pattern perpendicular to the center line. This will become the stitching line. Center the pattern on the chair seat with the pressed fold even with the chair back and smooth the fabric in place. Pin out excess fabric at the front corners, forming darts. Mark the dart seam lines with a pencil.

6. Mark dots on the front of the chair back pattern and on the fold of the chair seat pattern where the patterns meet at the outer edges of the seat back. Cut straight up from the bottom to the dots on the front chair back piece, allowing the fabric to spread so the side can be smoothed downward and the center bottom between dots can be smoothed forward under the seat pattern.

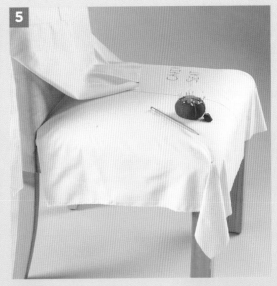

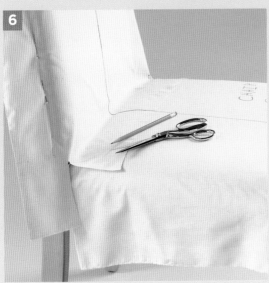

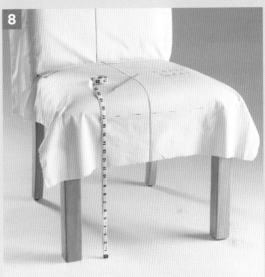

7. Pin the seat pattern to the front chair back pattern at the sides. Mark the seam on the front chair back piece between dots, even with the fold of the seat pattern. Continue marking the seam line down the sides of the front chair back even with the fold of the seat pattern.

8. Measure the distance from the floor to where the seat cushion meets the frame at the chair front. Record the measurement. Mark a seam line on the patterns all around the chair at this height from the floor.

9. Remove the patterns from the chair and redraw seam lines as necessary. Reposition the patterns on the chair; adjust as necessary. Add ½" (1.3 cm) seam allowances to all pattern pieces. Cut out the patterns.

Continued >>

Sewing the slipcover

1. Using the muslin patterns, cut one of each piece from the decorator fabric, matching the fabric design across seams, if necessary. Transfer all markings.

2. Staystitch the lower corners of the front piece, pivoting at the dots. Clip up to, but not through, the stitched corner.

3. Stitch darts on the front corners of the chair seat. Trim the excess fabric ¼" (6 mm) from the stitching, and press the seam allowances open.

4. Pin the chair seat to the front, matching the dots and lower edges. Stitch ½" (1.3 cm) seam. *Finish* the seam allowances and press them open.

5. Pin the front/seat to the back at the sides and top. Stitch. Using a ½" (1.3 cm) seam, stitch the chair front and back together across the top and down the sides. Finish the seam allowances and press them open.

6. If welting is desired, cut bias strips 1⅝" (4 cm) wide. The length of the welting is equal to the circumference of the lower edge of the slipcover. Make and apply welting as on page 110.

7. Measure the lower edge of the slipcover between the front darts. Add 14" (35.5 cm) for seam and pleat allowances to determine the width of the front skirt piece. Repeat for the sides, measuring from the dart to the side seam. Repeat for the back, measuring between side seams. To determine the length of the skirt pieces, double the measurement you recorded in step 8 of making the pattern, and add 1" (2.5 cm). At this length, the skirt will brush the floor. Adjust the measurement if you want it shorter. Cut the four skirt pieces.

8. Stitch the skirt pieces together into a circle, using ½" (1.3 cm) seams. Press the seam allowances open. Fold the skirt in half cross-wise, wrong sides together. Baste the upper edges together within the ½" (1.3 cm) seam allowance.

9. Mark with pins 6½" (16.3 cm) on each side of one of the skirt seams. Fold the skirt at the pin marks and bring the folds to the seam to form an inverted box pleat. Pin the pleat in place. Repeat at the three remaining seams.

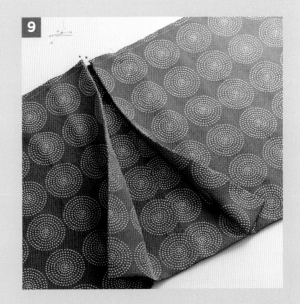

10. Check the fit of the skirt; adjust the sizes of the pleats if necessary. Baste across the tops of the pleats within the ½" (1.3 cm) seam allowance. Baste the skirt to the chair seat and back, right sides together. Place the slipcover on the chair and check the length of the skirt. Adjust if necessary. Stitch ½" (1.3 cm) seam. Finish the seam allowances together, and press them away from the skirt.

Tip

It is usually impossible to match a fabric pattern across all the seams in a slipcover. Match the pattern in the areas that are most visible, such as the seam between the seat and chair back and the seam between the seat front and the skirt front.

Ottoman

Rectangular ottomans with attached cushions are often used with upholstered chairs and sofas. Their styling is so basic that they easily blend with various furniture styles. This slipcover features a tailored skirt with inverted box pleats at the corners.

What you'll need

- [+] Decorator fabric
- [+] Lining
- [+] Decorator fabric for welting
- [+] Cording for welting

What you need to know

This skirted slipcover is suitable for an ottoman that has short legs or bun feet, with or without a skirt. Pin-fitting with muslin isn't necessary because all the pieces are rectangular and easily measured with a tape measure. The top and boxing strip are welted in the same dimensions as the ottoman itself. A hidden lip of fabric that extends from the boxing strip under the skirt helps you pull the cover firmly into place. Twill-tape ties sewn to this lip are tied around the legs to keep the slipcover from sliding up. The skirt is lined for body and to avoid a noticeable hem around the bottom.

Cutting Directions

- Measure the top of the ottoman from seam to seam. Add 1" (2.5 cm) in both directions for seam allowances, and cut a rectangle of fabric for the slipcover top.

- Measure the width of the ottoman boxing strip from seam to seam. Add ½" (1.3 cm) for the upper seam allowance and 1½" (3.8 cm) for the lower extension. The finished length of the slipcover boxing strip equals the circumference of the ottoman. You will have to seam the boxing strip in two equal pieces, so divide this measurement in half and add 1" (2.5 cm) for seam allowances. Cut the boxing strip pieces on the crosswise grain of the fabric, matching the print to one side of the slipcover top, if necessary.

- Measure for the skirt length from the lower seam of the ottoman boxing strip to the floor. (If the ottoman usually stands on carpet, measure on carpet for accuracy.) Add 2½" (6.5 cm) to this measurement for the cut length of the skirt. Cut four skirt pieces, one for each side, with the widths equal to the cut sides of the ottoman top plus 16" (40.5 cm).

- Cut lining pieces the same widths as the skirt pieces and 2" (5 cm) shorter than the skirt pieces.

- Cut bias fabric strips for the welting (page 110) with the length equal to twice the circumference of the ottoman plus additional length for seaming strips, joining ends, and inconspicuously positioning seams.

Sewing the Slipcover

1. Make welting as on page 110. Stitch the welting around the outer edge of the slip-cover top, following the continuous circle method.

2. Sew the boxing strip pieces together in ½" (1.3 cm) seams. Finish the lower edge of the boxing strip with zigzag stitches or serging. Pin the boxing strip to the slipcover top, matching the print on one side, if necessary. Clip into the boxing strip seam allowance at the corners to allow the fabric to spread. Stitch the boxing strip to the top, using a welting foot or zipper foot.

3. Mark a chalk line 1" (2.5 cm) from the lower edge of the boxing strip. Stitch the welting in a continuous circle to the boxing strip, aligning the raw edges of the welting to the marked line. Mark the lower edge of the boxing strip at the corners, even with the pivot points of the stitching on the top edge.

4. Sew the skirt pieces together in a big circle, using ½" (1.3 cm) seam allowances. Repeat for the lining pieces. Press the seam allowances open.

5. Pin the lower edges of the skirt and lining right side together, matching seams. Stitch ½" (1.3 cm) from the edges. Press the seam allowances toward the lining.

Continued >>

6. Fold the lining and skirt, wrong sides together, aligning the upper edges. Press. Baste the upper edges together.

7. At the upper edge of the skirt, at each seam, place a pin 1" (2.5 cm) to the left of the seam, a second pin 7" (18 cm) to the right of the seam, and a third pin 15" (38 cm) to the right of the seam. Fold each pleat, bringing the outer pin marks to the center pin mark; pin them in place. The seams will be hidden in the folds of the pleats.

8. Check the skirt for fit, and adjust the folds if necessary. Baste across the top of each pleat.

9. Pin the upper edge of the skirt over the welting at the lower edge of the boxing strip, right sides together, aligning the raw edges and matching the marks on the boxing strip to the centers of the pleats. Stitch, using a welting foot or zipper foot.

10. Cut eight lengths of twill tape, 18" (46 cm) long, for the ties. Stitch the ties to the extension of the boxing strip, 2" (5 cm) from each corner.

11. Place the slipcover on the ottoman, pulling on the boxing strip extension to position it snugly in place. Tie the ties behind the ottoman legs to keep the slipcover in place.

Tip *If your ottoman has casters, very short feet, or none at all, ties are impractical. Secure the slipcover by inserting screw pins through the boxing strip extension into the upholstered sides of the ottoman.*

Fitted Covers for Upholstered Furniture

Close-fitting slipcovers work well on fully upholstered armchairs or sofas. A slipcover can be made from a single fabric or several coordinating fabrics. For interest and stability, add contrasting welting in the seams. Make the skirt fully gathered or box-pleated to suit your taste.

What you'll need

- + Muslin for making patterns
- + Decorator fabric
- + Cording for welting
- + Zippers; one for chairs, two for sofas and love seats. The length of each zipper is 1" to 2" (2.5 to 5 cm) shorter than the length of the vertical seam at the side of the outside back. Additional zippers are needed for cushions (page 53).
- + Upholstery batting, if necessary, to pad existing furniture
- + Polyurethane foam cut in 2" (5 cm) strips to insert at sides and back
- + T-pins, tacks, or heavy-duty stapler and staples, for securing tacking strip to furniture

● ● ▨

What you need to know

A frequent concern about a slipcover is whether it will stay in place. To help secure the slipcover, an attached fabric strip, concealed under the skirt, is pinned to the existing fabric. Also, polyurethane foam pieces are tucked along the sides of the deck to provide a tight fit.

Furniture with a concave back design, such as a channel back or barrel back, is difficult to slipcover, and the slipcover may not fit well. For best results, a concave back should be wrapped or covered in a thick upholstery batting before it is slipcovered. Furniture with a tufted back or button back can be slipcovered, but the tufting and buttons are eliminated in the slipcover. The back is wrapped with upholstery batting to fill it out for a smooth fitting slipcover.

Making patterns for fitted slipcovers

The easiest way to make a slipcover pattern is by pin-fitting muslin on the chair or sofa. Before you start, look carefully at the furniture. Usually the seams in the slipcover will be in the same locations as the seams on the existing cover, but you may be able to add or eliminate some details, if it will not affect the fit of the slipcover. For example, if the existing cushions are waterfall style (wrapped in one piece from front to back), you can slipcover them as box cushions with welting. Or a chair with a pleated front arm can be slipcovered with a separate flat front arm piece.

The style of the skirt can also be changed. You may want to gather a skirt all the way around the furniture, allowing double fullness. Or you may want bunched gathers at the corners of a chair, or at the corners and center front of a sofa. For a more tailored look, the skirt can have box pleats instead of gathers.

A chair with rolled arms and loose back and seat cushions is used in the instructions that follow. This example includes the details that are common to most furniture. Although your furniture style may be different, use these basic steps as a guide.

Pin-fitting the pattern for the back

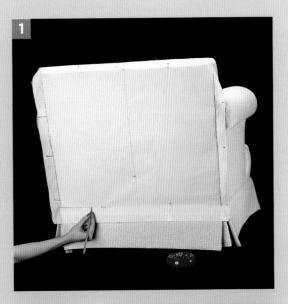

1. Remove the cushions. Measure the outside back of your chair or sofa between seam lines; cut muslin 3" to 4" (7.5 to 10 cm) larger than measurements. Mark a center line on the outside back piece, following the lengthwise grain. Pin the muslin piece to the chair, smoothing fabric; mark seam lines.

2. Measure the inside back between seam lines; cut muslin 15" (38 cm) wider and about 10" (25.5 cm) longer than measurements. This allows for 6" (15 cm) at the lower edge to tuck into the deck and hold the slipcover in place. Mark a center line on the inside back piece, following lengthwise grain.

3. Pin the outside back and inside back together along the top of the chair or sofa, matching center lines. Fold out excess fabric on the inside back piece at upper corner, forming a dart. Pin the muslin snugly, but do not pull the fabric tight.

4. Trim excess fabric on sides of the inside back to 2" (5 cm); clip along the arms as necessary for smooth curve. Push about ½" (1.3 cm) of fabric into crevices on sides and lower edge of the inside back; mark seam lines by pushing a pencil into crevices.

Pin-fitting the pattern for a pleated arm

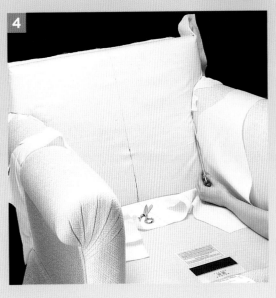

1. Measure the outside arm between seam lines; cut muslin 3" (7.5 cm) larger than measurements. Mark lengthwise grain line on the muslin. Pin the outside arm in place, with the grain line perpendicular to the floor and lower edge extending ½" (1.3 cm) beyond the seam line at the upper edge of the skirt. Smooth the fabric upward; pin. Pin the outside arm to the outside back. Mark the seam lines.

Continued >>

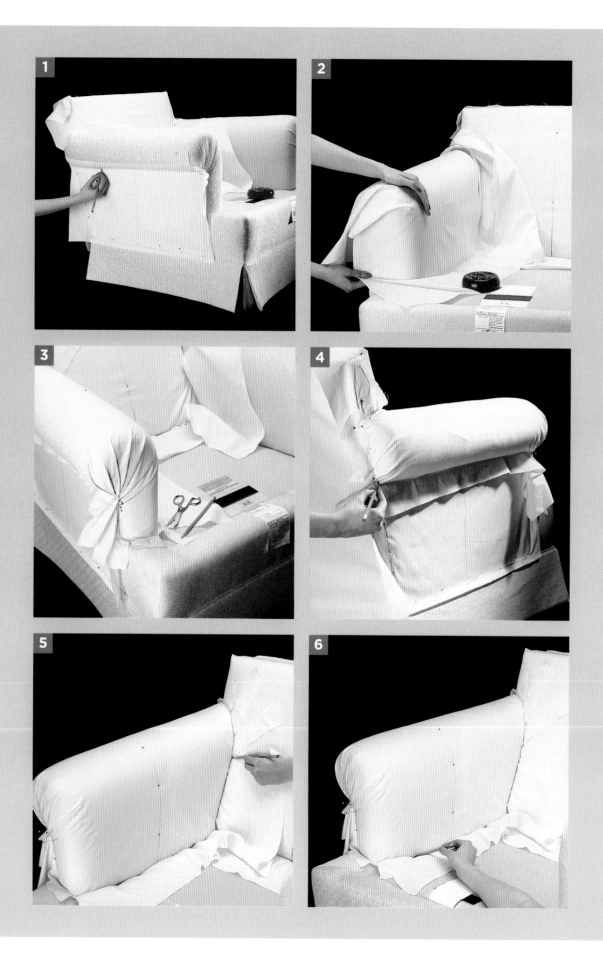

2. Measure the inside arm from deck to seam line at the upper edge of the outside arm, and from the inside back to the front of the arm; cut muslin about 9" (23 cm) larger than measurements. Mark lengthwise grain line on the muslin. Pin the inside arm piece in place, with 7" (18 cm) extending at inside back and grain line straight across the arm, smoothing fabric up and around the arm.

3. Pin the inside arm to the outside arm at front; clip and trim fabric at the front lower edge as necessary for a smooth fit. Pleat out fabric for the rolled arm to duplicate pleats in the existing fabric. Mark radiating fold lines of pleats.

4. Make tucks on the inside arm at the back of the chair, to fold out excess fabric; clip the inside arm as necessary for a smooth fit. Mark seam line at beginning and end of tucks on the inside arm and outside back.

5. Mark the inside arm and inside back with large dots, about halfway up the arm. Push about ½" (1.3 cm) of fabric on the inside arm into crevices at the deck and back.

6. Mark all seam lines on the muslin, smoothing fabric as you go.

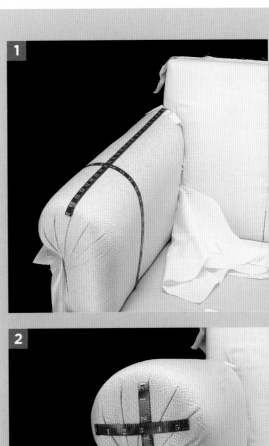

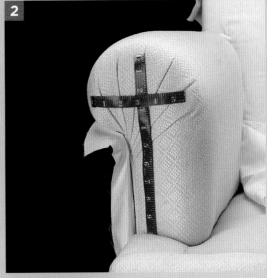

Pin-fitting the pattern for an arm with a front section

1. Follow page 39, step 1, for outside arm. Measure the inside arm from deck to seam line at the upper edge of the outside arm, and from the inside back to the front edge of the arm; cut muslin about 9" (23 cm) larger than these measurements. Mark lengthwise grain line on the muslin.

2. Measure front of the arm; cut muslin 2" to 3" (5 to 7.5 cm) larger than measurements. Mark lengthwise grain line on the muslin.

Continued >>

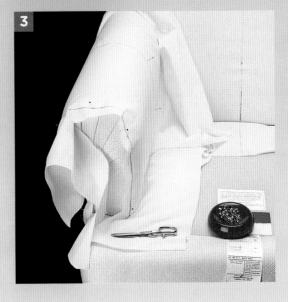

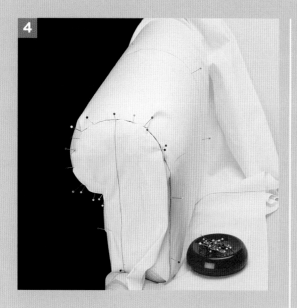

3. Pin the inside arm piece in place, with 7" (18 cm) extending at the inside back and grain line straight across the arm, smoothing fabric up and around the arm. Mark seam line at front edge of the arm; trim away excess fabric not needed for seam allowances.

4. Pin the front arm piece in place. Fold out excess fabric on the inside arm as necessary to fit the front arm piece, making two pleats. Mark seam line for the curve of the arm, following existing seam line on the chair. Complete the pattern as on page 41, steps 4, 5, and 6.

Pin-fitting the pattern for the deck

1. Measure the width at the deck front; measure the deck length, down the front of the chair to the skirt seam; cut muslin about 15" (38 cm) wider and 9" (23 cm) longer than these measurements. Mark a center line on the muslin, following the grain. Mark a seam line on the muslin at front edge on straight grain, ½" (1.3 cm) from the raw edge.

2. Pin the marked line on the muslin to the welting of the skirt seam, with center line centered on the skirt. Smooth muslin over the front edge and deck, and match center lines of deck and back.

3. Mark the deck and inside arm pieces with large dots, at the point where the deck meets the front of the inside arm. For furniture with T-cushion, clip excess fabric to the dots. Fold out excess fabric on deck at the front corner, forming a dart; pin and mark.

4. Pin the deck to the outside arm piece at the side of the chair; mark the seam line. Do not fit the deck snug. Push about ½" (1.3 cm) of fabric into the crevices at the sides and back of the deck; mark seam lines by pushing a pencil into the crevices.

Tip

Keep the grain lines of the pattern pieces parallel or perpendicular to the floor to ensure proper fit of the slipcover and make it easier to match designs at seams.

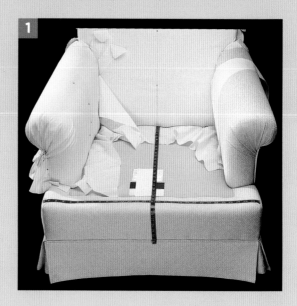

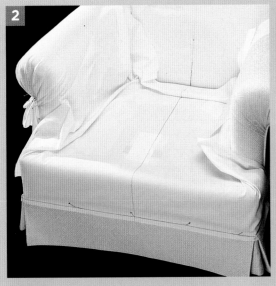

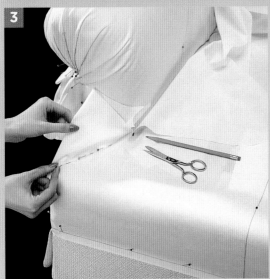

Pin-fitting the skirt

1. Measure for skirt around the sides, front, and back to determine the cut width of the skirt; allow for gathers or pleats. Plan seam placement, based on width of fabric and size of the furniture, so seams are concealed in gathers or pleats whenever possible; plan a seam at the back corner where the zipper will be inserted. Cut the number of fabric widths needed; cut muslin pieces 1" (2.5 cm) longer than length of the skirt.

2. Place raw edge of the muslin just below the lower edge of the skirt; pin at upper edge of the skirt, keeping muslin straight and even. Pin seams as you come to them; pin out full-ness for pleats or gathers. Pin vertical tucks in the skirt, pinning $1/8$" (3 mm) tuck near back corner on each side of the chair and $1/4$" (6 mm) tuck near each corner on back of the chair; tucks will be released in step 3 on page 44, adding ease to the skirt. Mark seams and placement of pleats or gathers.

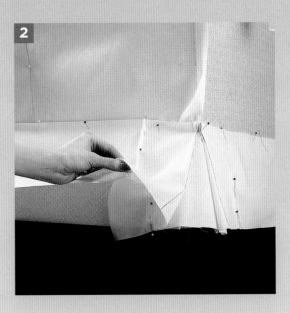

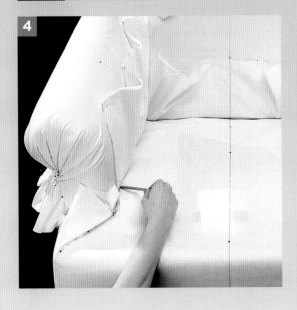

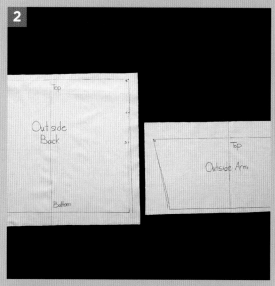

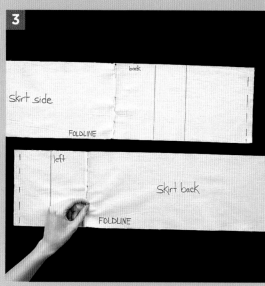

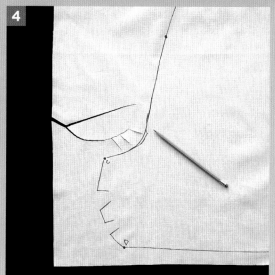

Preparing the pattern for cutting

1. Mark upper edge of all muslin pieces; label pieces. Check that all seam lines, darts, gathers, and pleats are marked. Mark dots at intersecting seams; label.

2. Remove the muslin. Add ¼" (6 mm) ease to back edge of the outside arm at lower corner. Add ½" (1.3 cm) ease to sides of the outside back at lower corners. Taper to the marked seam lines at upper corners.

3. Remove the pinned tucks near back corners of skirt pieces. Mark "fold line" at lower edge of the muslin for a self-lined skirt.

4. True straight seam lines, using a straightedge; true curved seam lines, drawing smooth curves. Do not mark seam lines in pleated areas.

5. Add 4" (10 cm) to lower edge of the inside back and back edge of deck.

6. Mark the lower edge of the inside arm from a point 4" (10 cm) away from seam line at the back edge to ½" (1.3 cm) from large dot at front edge; repeat for sides of the deck.

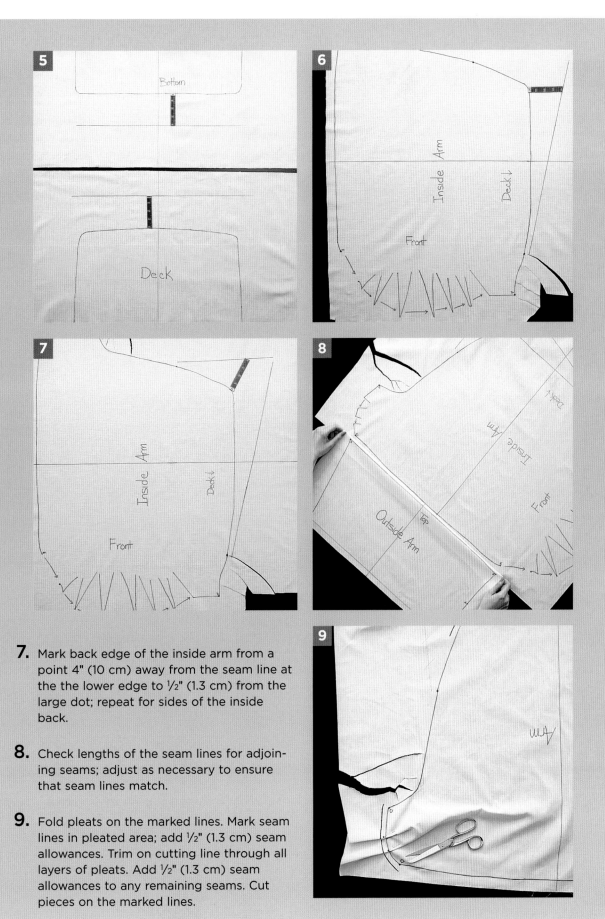

7. Mark back edge of the inside arm from a point 4" (10 cm) away from the seam line at the the lower edge to ½" (1.3 cm) from the large dot; repeat for sides of the inside back.

8. Check lengths of the seam lines for adjoining seams; adjust as necessary to ensure that seam lines match.

9. Fold pleats on the marked lines. Mark seam lines in pleated area; add ½" (1.3 cm) seam allowances. Trim on cutting line through all layers of pleats. Add ½" (1.3 cm) seam allowances to any remaining seams. Cut pieces on the marked lines.

Cutting directions

- Cut out the pieces, following the general guidelines on page 108.

- Cut a 3" (7.5 cm) tacking strip on the straight grain. This strip is used to secure the slipcover to the furniture with T-pins, tacks, or staples. Cut the length of the tacking strip equal to the distance around the furniture at the upper edge of the skirt.

Sewing the fitted slipcover

Although the slipcover for your furniture may be somewhat different from the style shown, many of the construction steps will be the same. It will be helpful to lay out the pieces and think through the sequence for sewing the seams of your slipcover. The labeled notches on adjoining seams will help you see how the pieces are to be joined together. To minimize handling of bulky quantities of fabric, stitch any small details, such as darts, before assembling the large pieces.

For durable seams, use a strong thread, such as long-staple polyester, and a medium stitch length of about 10 stitches per inch (2.5 cm). Because slipcovers have several thicknesses of fabric at intersecting seams with welting, use size 90/14 or 100/16 sewing needle.

Add welting to any seams that will be subjected to stress and wear, because welted seams are stronger than plain seams. For decorative detailing, welting can also be added to seams such as around the outside back and the upper edge of the skirt. On furniture with front arm pieces, welting is usually applied around the front of the arm as a design detail. See page 108 for instructions on making and applying welting.

For a chair, apply a zipper to one of the back seams of the slipcover. For a sofa, apply zippers to both back seams.

Sewing a fitted slipcover with a pleated front arm

1. Stitch darts at the upper corners of the inside back. If welting is desired, apply it to the upper front edges of the outside arm, pivoting at the corner.

2. Stitch darts at the outer front corners of the deck; stop stitching 1/2" (1.3 cm) from the raw edges at the inner corner.

3. Stitch the deck to the front of the arm and the inside arm; this can be stitched as two separate seams.

4. Pin pleats in place at the front and back of the arm. Check the fit over the arm of the chair. Baste in place on seam line.

5. Stitch the horizontal and vertical seams, joining the outside arm to inside arm; pivot at corner.

6. Pin the inside arms to inside back on both sides (1). Pin lower edge of the inside back to back edge of the deck (2). Make tucks in seams at the corners, if necessary, so pieces fit together. Stitch seams.

7. Apply welting around the sides and upper edge of slipcover unit (page 110); curve ends of the welting into seam allowance 1/2" (1.3 cm) from the lower edges (arrow). Join slipcover unit to outside back, leaving seam open for zipper application. Apply welting to the lower edge.

8. Stitch skirt pieces together, leaving seam at the back corner unstitched for zipper insertion; press seams open. Fold the skirt in half lengthwise, wrong sides together and press.

9. Press pleats for pleated skirt. For a gathered skirt, stitch gathering stitches by zigzagging over a cord; for a skirt with bunched gathers, stitch gathering stitches between the markings.

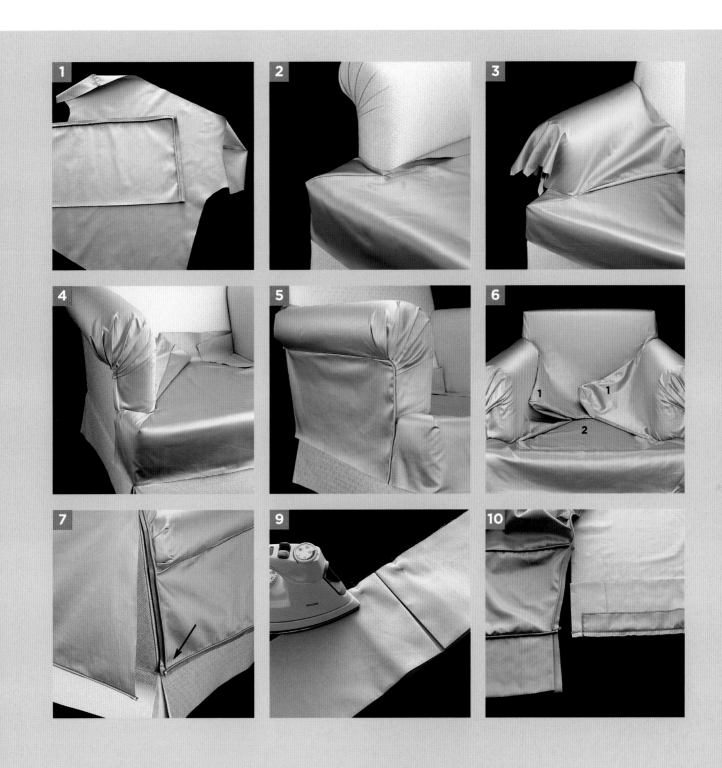

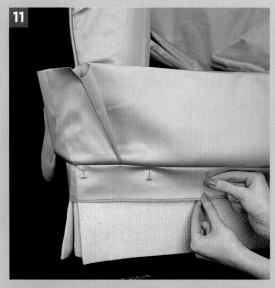

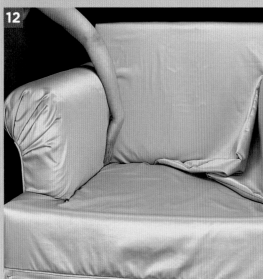

10. Pin the tacking strip to the upper edge of the skirt on the wrong side. Join the skirt to adjoining pieces; for a gathered skirt, pull the gathering threads together to fit. Apply the zipper (page 50). Sew cushion covers (pages 53 to 65).

11. Apply slipcover to furniture. Secure the tacking strip to the furniture by pinning into upholstery with T-pins.

12. Push extra fabric allowance into crevices around the deck and inside back. Stuff 2" (5 cm) strips of polyurethane foam into crevices around the deck to keep fabric from pulling out. Insert the cushions.

Sewing a fitted slipcover with a front arm piece

1. Stitch darts at the upper corners of the inside back. Apply welting to the upper edge of the inside arm, if desired. Stitch the horizontal seam, joining the outside arm to the inside arm. Pin and baste tucks at the front edge of the inside/outside arm.

2. Stitch the front arm piece to the front edge of the inside/outside arm; stop stitching 2" (5 cm) from the outer end of the front arm piece.

3. Follow steps 2 and 3 on page 46. Pin the pleats in place at the back of the arm; baste in place on the seam line.

4. Complete the vertical seam at the front edge of the outside arm. Finish the slipcover as in steps 6 to 12 on pages 46 and 48.

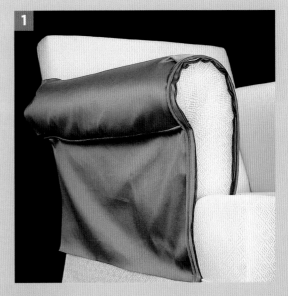

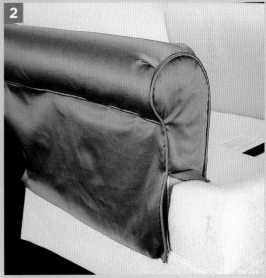

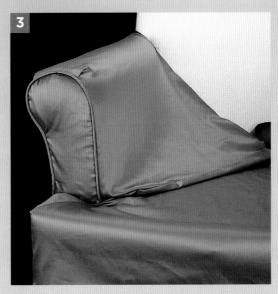

49

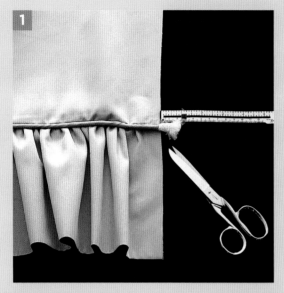

Applying the zipper

1. Pull the cording out slightly from the ends of the skirt opening; trim off the ends 1" (2.5 cm). Pull the seam to return the cording to its original position.

2. Press under the seam allowances on the zipper opening. Place the open zipper on the welted side of the seam, so the welting just covers the zipper teeth and with the zipper tab at the lower edge. Pin in place; fold in the seam allowance at the lower edge of the skirt to miter. Fold up the end of the zipper tape.

3. Edgestitch on the skirt, using a zipper foot, with the zipper teeth positioned close to the folded edge. Stitch in the ditch of the welted seam.

4. Close the zipper. Place the remaining side of the zipper under the seam allowance, with the folded edge at the welted seam line. Pin in place; fold in the seam allowance at the lower edge of the skirt to miter. Fold up the end of the zipper tape.

5. Open the zipper. Stitch ⅜" (1 cm) from the folded edge, pivoting at the top of the zipper.

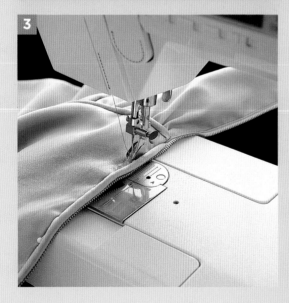

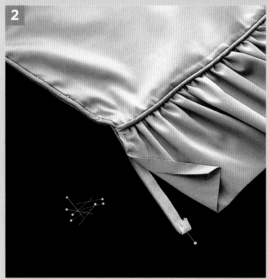

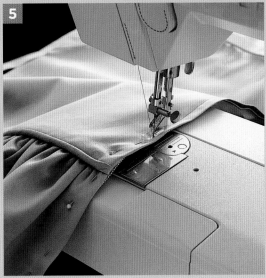

Pleated skirt

1. Follow steps 1 to 5, opposite, except break the stitching at the upper edge of the skirt. On the skirt, stitch through the lower layer of the box pleat; stitch as close as possible to the seam at the upper edge of the skirt.

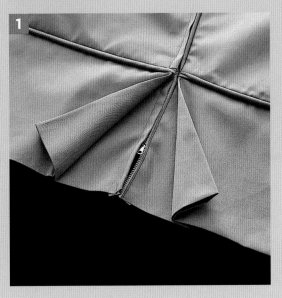

Cushions

You can make slipcovers for cushions on benches or window seats, as well as for those on sofas or chairs. Most cushions fall into one of the three styles shown at left: knife-edge (top), waterfall (middle), and boxed (bottom). Any of these styles can be fitted flush to the front of the chair or T-shaped, wrapping around the front of the chair arms.

What you'll need

- + Muslin for making patterns
- + Decorator fabric
- + Zipper, about 8" (20.5 cm) longer than back edge of cushion
- + Fabric and cording for fabric-covered welting; or brush fringe or twisted welting
- + High-density polyurethane foam, for making new cushion inserts
- + Electric knife, optional
- + Polyester upholstery batting, for making new cushion inserts
- + Foam adhesive or hand needle and heavy thread, for making new cushion inserts
- + Large plastic bag or sheet of plastic
- + Vacuum cleaner with hose

What you need to know

To make it easier to insert the cushion, install a zipper across the back of the slipcover, extending about 4" (10 cm) onto each side. For cushions that are exposed on three sides, install a zipper across the back of the slipcover only. Use upholstery zippers, which are available in longer lengths than dressmaker zippers. For boxed and waterfall cushions, the tab of the zipper will be concealed in a pocket at the end of the zipper opening. This is an upholsterer's technique that gives a professional finish.

Boxed and knife-edge cushions can be sewn with or without welting at the seams. See page 110 for instructions on making and attaching welting. Knife-edge cushions on chairs or sofas usually have a welted seam around the center on sides where the cushion is exposed. If there are hidden sides, such as for a knife-edge seat cushion on a wing chair, the hidden sides are often constructed with a boxing strip. Waterfall cushions, more common in contemporary furniture, are sewn with one continuous piece of fabric wrapping over the front, from top to bottom. This style has a boxing strip around the sides and back and is usually made without welting.

Slipcovers for cushions can often be put on right over the existing upholstery fabric like the rest of the slipcover. There are circumstances, however, when it is better to remove the old cover and insert the cushion into the new slipcover. This is a better option if the slipcover fabric is lighter weight than the upholstery or if there is existing welting that will show through or cause wear on the new slipcover.

For the best fit, pin-fit muslin to the existing cushion to make a pattern for the new cushion cover.

Cutting directions

Knife-edge cushion

- If the cushion is rectangular, fairly flat, and soft, like a pillow, cut a cushion cover top to the same dimensions as the original cushion plus 1" (2.5 cm) for seam allowances. Cut the cushion cover bottom 1" (2.5 cm) longer than the top to allow for ½" (1.3 cm) seam allowances at the zipper closure.

- To cover a rectangular cushion that has a thick, firm, foam insert, cut a top and bottom with the width and length equal to the cushion width and length plus the foam depth plus 1" (2.5 cm) for seam allowances.

- If continuous zipper tape is used, cut the zipper tape with the length equal to at least three-fourths of the cushion width, or purchase a conventional zipper with this approximate length.

- Cut fabric strips for the welting long enough to fit the welted section of the cushion.

Boxed cushion

- Cut the top and bottom pieces 1" (2.5 cm) larger than the cushion size to allow for seam allowances. For boxed T-cushions, pin-fit a muslin pattern to ensure accurate cutting.

- Measure the original boxing strip between seams and add 1" (2.5 cm) for seam allowances. Cut the boxing strip with the length equal to the total measurement of the front and sides of the cushion. Excess length will be cut off during construction. If piecing is necessary, allow 1" (2.5 cm) for each seam, planning the placement of the seams out of view along the sides of the cushion.

- If continuous zipper tape is used, cut the zipper tape 8" (20.5 cm) longer than the back cushion measurement, or purchase an upholstery zipper with this approximate length. Cut two fabric strips for the zipper closure with the length equal to the length of the zipper tape and the width equal to half the cut width of the boxing strip plus ¾" (2 cm).

- If the cushion will be welted, cut fabric strips for the welting (page 110) with the length equal to twice the circumference of the cushion plus additional length for seaming strips, joining ends, and inconspicuously positioning seams.

Waterfall cushion

- Pin-fit a muslin pattern for the continuous top/bottom piece. Cut a cushion top and bottom piece, using the pattern. Mark the end of the piece that will become the cushion top (with a directional print or napped fabric, the fabric will run in the correct direction only on the top).

- Cut the side boxing strips. Measure the original boxing strip between the seams and add 1" (2.5 cm) for seam allowances. Cut each boxing strip with the length equal to the side measurement of the cushion plus 1" (2.5 cm). Excess length will be cut off during construction.

- If continuous zipper tape is used, cut the zipper tape with the length equal to the back cushion measurement plus 8" (20.5 cm), or purchase an upholstery zipper with this approximate length. Cut two fabric strips for the zipper closure, with the length equal to the length of the zipper tape and the width equal to half the cut width of the boxing strip plus ¾" (2 cm).

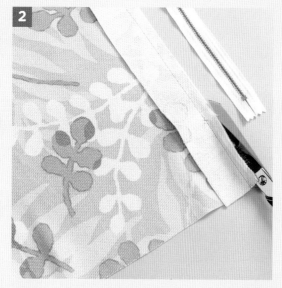

Sewing a knife-edge cushion cover

1. Fold in the lower edge of the cushion back 1¾" (4.5 cm), right sides together; press. Place the zipper alongside the fold and mark the fold at the location of the zipper stops. Stitch ½" (1.3 cm) from the fold, from the side to the first mark; backstitch. Machine-baste to the second mark; backstitch, then finish the seam to the opposite edge.

2. Cut on the fold. Press the seam allowances open.

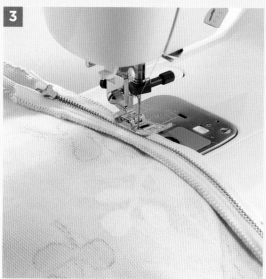

3. Center the closed zipper facedown over the seam, with the stops at the marks. Glue-baste or pin the zipper tape to the seam allowances only. Finish the seam allowances, catching the zipper tape in the stitches.

4. Spread the cushion cover back flat, right side up. Mark the top and bottom of the zipper coil with pins. Center a strip of ½" (1.3 cm) transparent tape over the seam from pin to pin. Topstitch a narrow rectangle along the edges of the tape, using a zipper foot. Stitch slowly as you cross the zipper just beyond the stops. Remove the tape. Pull threads to the underside and knot. Remove the basting stitches.

5. Make welting as on page 110. Sew the welting around the outer edge of the cushion cover top, following the continuous circle method.

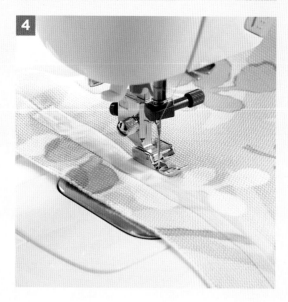

6. Open the zipper partially. Pin the cover top and bottom right sides together. With the wrong side of the top facing up, stitch just inside the first welting stitches, crowding the cording.

7. Turn the cover right side out through the zipper opening.

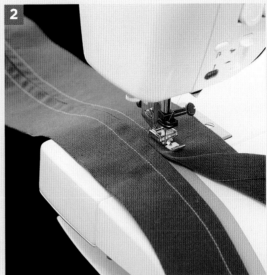

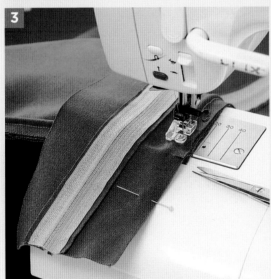

Sewing a rectangular boxed cushion cover

1. Make welting as on page 110. Sew the welting around the outer edge of the cushion top and cushion bottom, following the continuous circle method.

2. Press under ³/₄" (2 cm) seam allowance on one long edge of the zipper strip. Position the folded edge of the strip along the center of the zipper teeth, right side up. Using a zipper foot, topstitch ³/₈" (1 cm) from the fold. Repeat for the opposite side, making sure folds meet at the center of the zipper.

If using continuous zipper tape, attach the zipper pull to the tape.

3. Center the zipper strip over the back edge of the cushion top, right sides together. Stitch the zipper strip to the cushion top, beginning and ending on the sides about 1½" (3.8 cm) beyond the corners. Clip into the zipper strip seam allowance at each corner to allow the fabric to spread, and pivot.

4. Align the center of the boxing strip to the front center of the cushion top, matching the print, if necessary; pin-mark the pieces separately. Smooth the boxing strip to the right front corner; mark with a ³/₈" (1 cm)

Continued >>

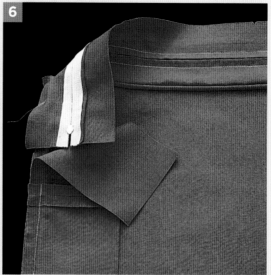

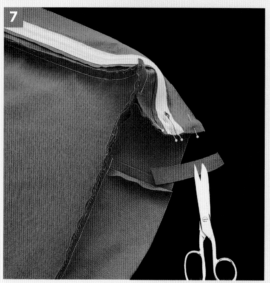

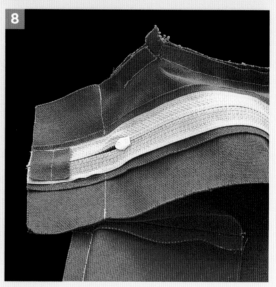

clip into the seam allowance. Smooth the boxing strip along the right side of the cushion top; pin the boxing strip to the cushion top about 6" (15 cm) from the back corner.

5. Stitch the boxing strip to the cushion top, beginning at the side pin and sewing ½" (1.3 cm) seam. For a welted cover, use a welting foot or zipper foot. Match the clip mark to the front corner; pivot the stitching at the corner.

6. Continue stitching the boxing strip to the cushion top, matching the center marks. Clip once into the boxing strip seam allowance at the left front corner; pivot. Stop stitching

about 6" (15 cm) from the back left corner.

7. Cut the boxing strip 4" (10 cm) beyond the point where it overlaps the zipper pull end of the zipper strip. Pin the end of the boxing strip to the end of the zipper strip, right sides together, matching all cut edges.

8. Stitch together 2" (5 cm) from the end; pivot at the zipper tape. Stitch along the outer edge of the zipper tape to within ½" (1.3 cm) of the end; pivot. Place a small scrap of fabric over the zipper teeth. Stitch slowly across the teeth to the opposite side of the zipper tape, taking care not to break the needle; pivot. Stitch along the opposite

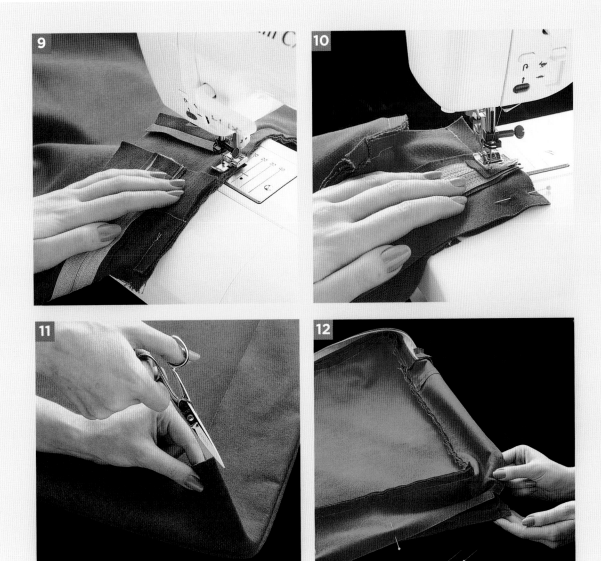

side of the zipper tape until 2" (5 cm) from the end; pivot, and stitch to the edge.

9. Finger-press the seam allowance toward the boxing strip. Finish sewing the zipper strip and boxing strip to the cushion top. A small pocket forms to hide the zipper pull when the cover is closed.

10. Cut the opposite end of the boxing strip 1" (2.5 cm) beyond the point where it overlaps the end of the zipper strip. Pin the ends together. Stitch ½" (1.3 cm) from the ends, placing a scrap of fabric over the zipper teeth and stitching slowly. Turn the seam

allowance toward the boxing strip. Finish sewing the zipper strip and boxing strip to the cushion top.

11. Fold the boxing strip straight across at the corner; mark the opposite side of the boxing strip with a ³⁄₈" (1 cm) clip into the seam allowance. Repeat for all the corners.

12. Open the zipper partially. Pin the boxing strip to the cushion bottom, matching the clip marks to the corners. Stitch. Turn the cover right side out through the zipper opening.

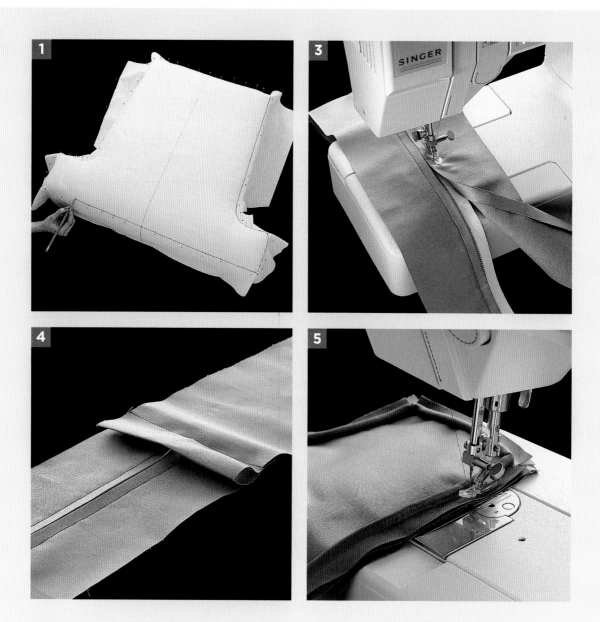

Sewing a boxed T-cushion cover

1. Cut muslin about 4" (10 cm) larger than the top of the cushion; mark the grain line at the center of the fabric. Place the muslin over the cushion; pin along the seam line, smoothing out the fabric. Mark the seam line along the pin marks.

2. Remove the muslin. True the seam lines, using a straightedge. Fold the muslin in half to check that the piece is symmetrical; make any necessary adjustments. Add ½" (1.3 cm)

seam allowances to the pattern. Cut the pieces as in the cutting directions (page 55).

3. Press under a ½" (1.3 cm) seam allowance on one long edge of each zipper strip. Position the folded edges of the strips along the center of the zipper teeth, right sides up. Using a zipper foot, topstitch ⅜" (1 cm) from folds.

4. Press under 2" (5 cm) on one short end of the boxing strip. Lap the boxing strip over the zipper strip to cover the zipper tab. Stitch through all layers 1½" (3.8 cm) from the folded edge of the boxing strip.

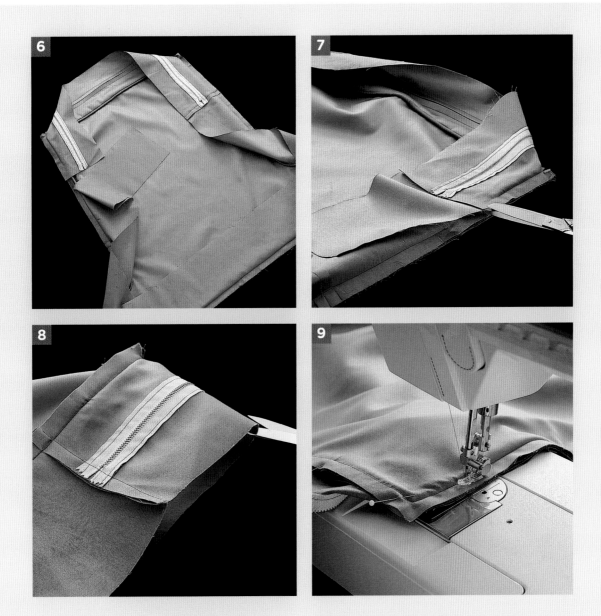

5. Make and apply welting as on page 110. Stitch welting to the right side of top and bottom pieces.

6. Place the boxing strip on the slipcover top, right sides together; center the zipper on the back edge. Start stitching 2" (5 cm) from the zipper end, crowding the cording. Clip the corners as you come to them; stop stitching 4" (10 cm) from the starting point.

7. Clip to mark the seam allowances at the ends of the boxing strip. Stitch the boxing strip ends together. Trim off excess fabric; finger-press the seam open. Finish stitching the boxing strip to the slipcover top.

8. Fold the boxing strip, and clip the seam allowance to mark the lower corners; be sure all corners are aligned with the corners on the slipcover top. Open the zipper.

9. Place the boxing strip and slipcover bottom right sides together. Match the clips of the boxing strip to the corners of the slipcover bottom; stitch. Turn the cover right side out.

10. Fold the cushion to insert it into the cover. Stretch the cover from front to back. Close the zipper. Smooth the cover from center to edges. Stretch the welting taut from corner to corner to square the cushion.

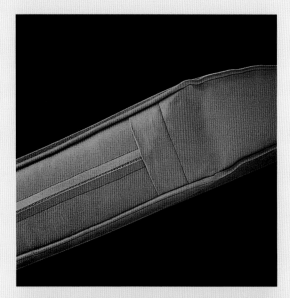

Alternative zipper placement (left). Install the zipper across the back of the slipcover, without extending it around the sides, if the slipcover will be exposed on three sides.

Matching patterned fabric

1. Cut the slipcover top and boxing strips so the pattern matches at the front seam lines. Notch the front corners on the upper and lower edges of the boxing strip.

2. Stitch the boxing strip to the front edge of the slipcover top first. Then continue stitching the boxing strip to the slipcover top and bottom.

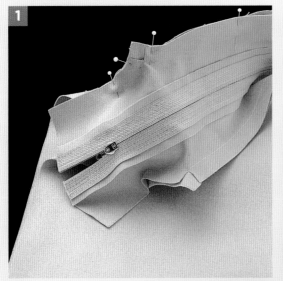

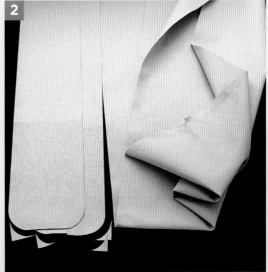

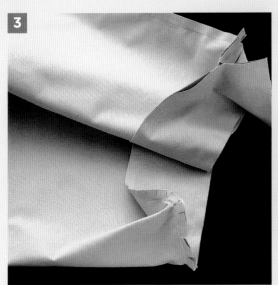

Sewing a waterfall cushion cover

1. Follow steps 2 and 3 for the box cushion on page 57. Fold the zipper strip straight across at the corner; mark the opposite edge with a ³⁄₈" (1 cm) clip into the seam allowance. Repeat at the other corner. Pin the zipper strip to the back edge of the cushion bottom, matching the clip marks to the corners. Stitch, beginning and ending about 1¹⁄₂" (3.8 cm) beyond the corners.

2. Mark the center of the front short end of each side of the boxing strip; round the front corners of the side boxing strips slightly. Mark the outer edges of the top/bottom cushion at the center front. Staystitch a scant ¹⁄₂" (1.3 cm) from the outer edges of the top/bottom piece a distance on either side of the marks equal to the cushion height.

3. Clip the seam allowances to the staystitching every ¹⁄₂" (1.3 cm). Pin the side boxing strip to the top/bottom, right sides together, aligning the center marks. Check to see that corresponding points on the top/bottom match up directly across from each other on the boxing strip. Sew ¹⁄₂" (1.3 cm) seam, beginning and ending 6" (15 cm) from the back corners. Repeat on the opposite side.

Continued >>

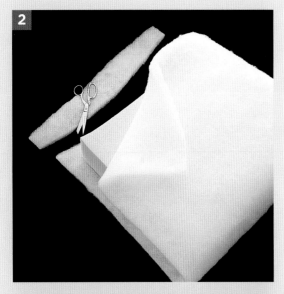

4. Follow steps 7 to 10 on pages 58 and 59. Open the zipper partially. Finish sewing the boxing strip to the top/bottom on both sides. Turn the cushion cover right side out through the zipper opening.

Making a new cushion insert

1. Cut foam to the finished size and shape of the cushion, using an electric knife. Hold the knife blade perpendicular to the foam to assure straight sides. Or take your measurements to the store and have the foam cut there.

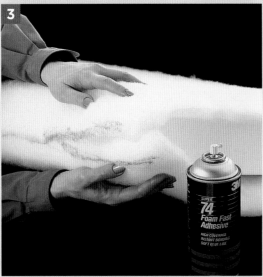

2. Wrap polyester batting over the foam from front to back. Trim the sides and back so that the cut edges overlap about 1" (2.5 cm) at the center of the cushion.

3. Apply spray foam adhesive to the cut edges of the batting and the back of the cushion. Overlap the edges, and press them firmly together to seal. Or whipstitch the edges together, using a large needle and heavy thread. Repeat for the sides.

4. Trim excess batting vertically at the corners. Apply adhesive, and press the edges together to seal. Or whipstitch the corners in place.

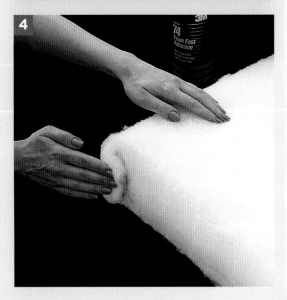

5. Fold the cushion in half from front to back. Insert the cushion into the opening, and gradually work it toward the front of the cover (or use the vacuum method at right). Stretch the cover to fit the cushion. Check to see that the cushion is inserted symmetrically, with equal fullness on both sides. Turn the seam allowances toward the boxing strip all around the cushion. Zip the cover closed, hiding the zipper pull in the pocket.

Vacuum method for inserting the cushion

1. Insert the prepared cushion into a lightweight trash bag or wrap it with lightweight plastic. Overlap the open edge of the plastic at one end. Insert the vacuum hose into a small hole cut in the plastic or wrap the plastic around the hose and hold tightly.

2. Press the end of the hose against the cushion. Turn on the vacuum. Suck air from the cushion until it slips easily into the cover. Turn off the vacuum and remove the plastic, allowing air to reenter the cushion.

Wing Chair

The wing chair, a mainstay in many traditional living rooms, is often the preferred chair in the room. With its high back and extended sides, the wing chair can be very cozy and comfortable. So when it's time to change the room's décor, a slipcover updates the look and lets you keep your favorite chair.

What you'll need

- Muslin for making patterns
- Decorator fabric
- Contrasting fabric for welting, optional
- Cording for welting
- Interfacing
- Zipper, about 8" (20.5 cm) longer than back edge of cushion
- Upholstery batting, if necessary, to pad the existing furniture
- Polyurethane foam, 2" (5 cm) strips to insert at the sides and back of deck
- T-pins, tacks, or heavy-duty stapler and staples, for securing tacking strip to furniture
- Button kit and six or seven button forms for covered buttons, or six or seven decorator buttons

What you need to know

The basic instructions for slipcovering a wing chair are the same as for the fitted slipcover shown on page 36, with a few modifications for the wings of the chair. This slipcover is designed with a center back button and buttonhole closure. If you prefer a zipper, simply follow the directions for the fitted slipcover (page 37).

Many wing chairs have exposed legs that are decorative, and you may wish to leave them exposed. If the legs are decorative or protrude away from the chair, making a long skirt unsuitable, make a short, self-lined gathered or box-pleated skirt.

Pin-fitting a slipcover for a wing chair

1. Pin-fit the pattern for the inside and outside back as on page 39, steps 1 and 2; in step 1, mark a line 2" (5 cm) to the right and left corner, for overlap and underlap at the back center opening and, in step 2, cut muslin 8" (20.5 cm) wider, not 15" (38 cm). Mark a line for the upper edge of the skirt.

2. Measure the length of the inside wing from the seam line at the top to the seam line at the top of the arm, and measure the width of the inside wing from the inside back across the wing at the widest point around the front to the seam line; add to this measurement the distance from the inside back to the outside back, measured across the top of the chair at the inside wing. Cut muslin about 6" (15 cm) wider and 4" (10 cm) longer than measurements. Mark the lengthwise grain line on the inside wing piece perpendicular to the floor.

3. Measure the length of the outside wing from the seam line at the top to the seam line along the arm, and measure the width of the wings across the widest point. Cut muslin about 4" (10 cm) wider and longer than measurements. Mark the lengthwise grain line on the outside wing piece.

4. Pin the inside back piece to the chair. Follow step 4 on page 39, omitting reference to clipping along the arms and sides. Continue to mark a line on the inside back piece at the top of the chair along seam line of the inside back and wing, and clip to marked line at the point where the top of the chair meets the inside back.

5. Pin the outside wing piece in place, with grain line perpendicular to the floor and with the lower edge extending ½" (1.3 cm) beyond the seam line aligning with the arm. Smooth fabric upward; pin the outside wing to the outside back; mark seam.

Continued >>

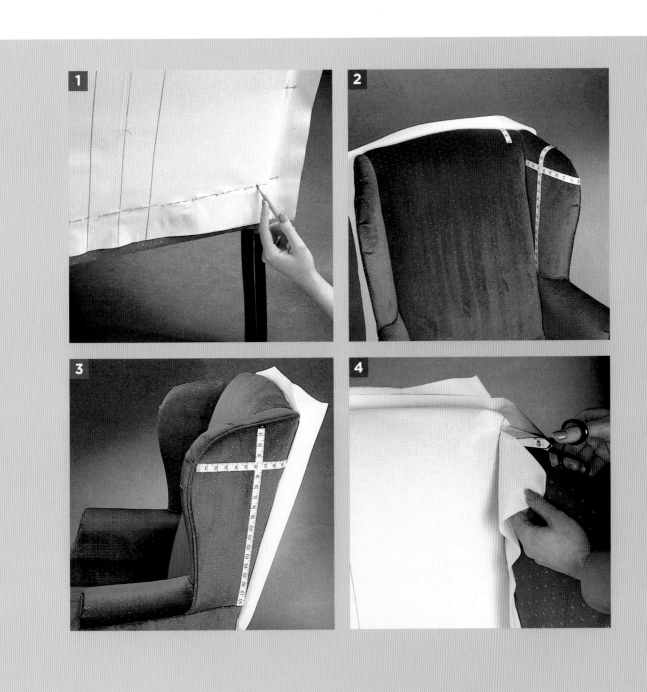

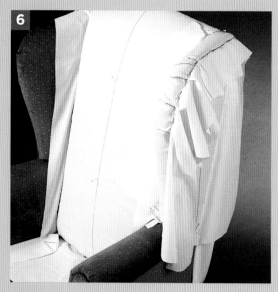

6. Pin the inside wing in place, with the grain line perpendicular to the floor and with the lower edge extending ½" (1.3 cm) beyond the seam line along the arm. Push the fabric into the crevice at inside back; mark seam line and clip as in step 4. Pin the inside back to the outside back. Pin the inside wing to the outside wing at front; clip and trim the fabric at lower edge as necessary for a smooth fit. Pleat out excess fabric around curve of the inside wing piece, duplicating pleats in existing fabric. Mark fold lines of the pleats. Mark all seam lines on the pinned edges.

7. Follow steps 1 to 6 on pages 39 and 41 for a chair with a pleated arm; in step 4, make tucks, if necessary at back of the arm where the arm meets the wing. Or follow steps 1 to 4 on pages 41 aand 42, for an arm with a front section.

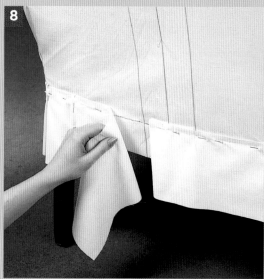

8. Follow page 42, steps 1 to 4, to pin-fit pattern for the deck. Pin-fit the skirt as on page 43, step 1; add 5" (12.7 cm) to each end of the skirt to allow for overlap, underlap, facings, and seam allowance at the center back closure and omit reference to seam at back corner for zipper. Follow page 43, step 2; if chair does not have a skirt, pin the skirt slipcover piece to the chair at marked upper skirt line, pinning ½" (1.3 cm) from upper raw edge of the skirt.

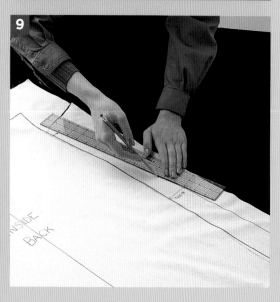

9. Follow page 44, step 1. Remove the muslin. True marked lines on the sides of the inside back piece. Insert a ruler into crevice at the top of the chair at the side of the inside back; record measurement for tuck-in. Repeat at the center and bottom along the side of the inside back. On sides of the inside back piece, mark points a distance from the marked line equal to tuck-in measurement at the top, center, and bottom. Draw a line connecting points. Mark points along the inside wing and inside arm pieces, corresponding to tuck-in points marked on the inside back. Draw line connecting these points.

10. On the outside back, cut on the marked line 2" (5 cm) to the right of the center line; discard remaining portion of the outside back piece. Follow page 44, steps 3 to 6; in step 3, mark 1/2" (1.3 cm) seam allowances at the ends, and mark fold lines 3½" (9 cm) from the ends for center back facings. Continue as on page 45, steps 8 and 9.

Sewing a slipcover for a wing chair with a pleated arm

1. Lay out and cut fabric for the slipcover as on pages 46 to 48, cutting a right and left back piece, using the outside back pattern. Cut two facing strips, 4" (10 cm) wide, for the center back with the length equal to measurement of the line at the center back. Align the long edges of the facing strips with the long edges of the outside back, and trim the upper edge of facing strips to match the outer back piece.

2. Apply welting to upper and front edges of the outside arm, if desired, pivoting at the corner. Follow page 46, steps 2 and 3. Pin the pleats in place around the inside wing. Check the fit over the wing of the chair. Baste in place on the seam line.

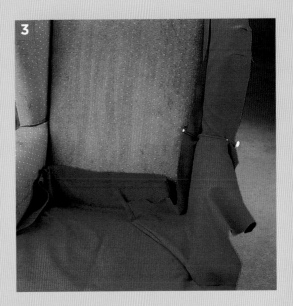

3. Staystitch a scant 1/2" (1.3 cm) from raw edges on the inside arm piece around the curve at the top of the arm; clip to stitching. Apply welting to the seam, if desired. Pin the lower edge of the inside wing to the top of the inside arm, right sides together; stitch from the inside back to 1/2" (1.3 cm) from the remaining side. Clip seam allowances.

Continued >>

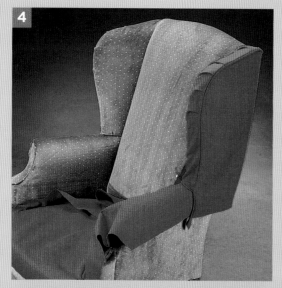

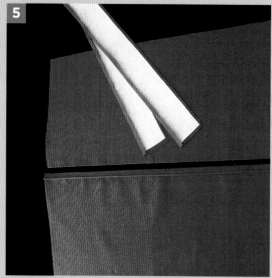

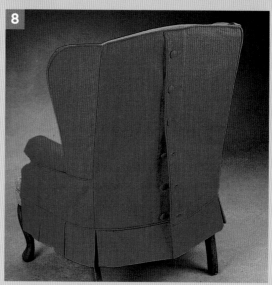

4. Stitch welting to the outside wing piece around the upper and front edges, if desired. Pin the inside wing and arm piece to the outside wing, right sides together; stitch around the upper and front edges from the seam line at the back to lower raw edge at the front.

5. Follow page 46, steps 4 to 6; in step 6, you will be pinning the inside wings and the inside arms to the inside back on both sides. Apply interfacing to the back facing pieces, within the seam allowances. Press under ½" (1.3 cm) along one long edge of the facing pieces. Apply welting to the left outside back piece, if desired.

6. Stitch the facing pieces to the outside back pieces, right sides together, using ½" (1.3 cm) seam allowances; press. Pin the facing to the outside back piece, wrong sides together; edge-stitch close to the fold. Repeat for the other piece. Lap the left outside back piece over the right outside back piece; baste across the upper edges. Continue as on page 46, step 7, omitting reference to leaving the seam open for the zipper.

7. Stitch the skirt pieces together; press the seams open. For a self-lined skirt, fold the skirt in half, right sides together. Stitch ½" (1.3 cm) from the raw edges at the ends; clip the corners. Turn the skirt right side out;

align the upper edges, and press. Turn under 3" (7.5 cm) on each end of the skirt for facing; press.

8. Follow pages 46 and 48, steps 9 and 10; in step 10, omit reference to the zipper. Mark placement of buttonholes on the left outside back piece, spacing evenly. Stitch the buttonholes. Stitch buttons to the right outside back piece at locations corresponding to the buttonholes. Continue as on page 48, steps 11 and 12.

Sewing a slipcover for a wing chair with a front arm piece

1. Follow step 1, page 71, for cutting and laying out the slipcover. Pin the pleats in place around the inside wing. Check fit over wing of the chair. Baste in place on the seam line. Follow steps 3 and 4, pages 71 and 72. Apply welting to the upper edge of the outside arm piece. Stitch a horizontal seam, joining the outside arm to the inside arm. Pin and baste tucks at the front edge of the inside/outside arm. Apply welting to the front edge of the inside/outside arm.

2. Follow page 49, steps 2 and 3. Complete the vertical seam at the front edge of the outside arm. Follow page 46, step 6; you will be pinning the inside wings and the inside arms to the inside back on both sides. Apply interfacing to the back facing pieces, within seam allowances. Press up ½" (1.3 cm) along one long edge of the facing pieces. Apply welting to the left outside back piece, if desired. Complete the slipcover, following steps 6 to 8, opposite and above.

Tip

If you intend to launder your slipcover occasionally, preshrink the fabric and choose polyester cording for the welting. If you must use cotton cording, tie it in a loose coil, dip it in hot water, place it in a mesh laundry bag, and dry it in a dryer before sewing the welting.

Futon Cover

A futon is affordable and multifunctional. It can easily be converted from a chair or sofa to a bed by changing the position of the futon frame from an upright to a reclining position. The futon mattress often comes with a fabric cover that is not only decorative, but also protects the mattress from becoming stained or worn. You can sew your own futon mattress cover that coordinates with the decorating scheme of the room.

What you'll need

- (+) Two flat cotton sheets, the same size as the futon mattress, or decorator fabric

- (+) Zipper, with the length of the zipper tape equal to combined length of the two ends and one side of the mattress plus 1" (2.5 cm)

● ● ○

What you need to know

For a cover without any seams on the front and back, use bed sheets. Select a solid-colored sheet or a patterned sheet with a nondirectional design. This allows you to turn the mattress regularly with the cover on, maintaining even wear on the cover as well as the mattress. Purchase 100% cotton sheets with a high thread count—the higher the count the more durable the cover will be. Two flat sheets the same size as the mattress provide enough fabric for all pieces of the cover. Before you cut the pieces, remove the stitching from the hems, then launder and press the sheets.

Make the cover so the lengthwise grain runs from the seat to the back, rather than from arm to arm. If you substitute a decorator fabric for the sheets, run the seams from the seat to the back.

For ease in inserting or removing the mattress, the cover is constructed with a zippered closure that extends along three sides.

Cutting directions

- Cut the front and back pieces for the futon cover, with the length and width of the pieces 1" (2.5 cm) longer and wider than the finished width of the futon cover. If you need to piece decorator fabric, run a full width of fabric up the center and add equal, partial widths at the sides of both the front and back.

- Cut one piece for the boxing strip that is 1" (2.5 cm) longer than the length of the futon cover and 1" (2.5 cm) wider than the thickness of the mattress. Cut one zipper tab, 4" (10 cm) long, with the cut width of the tab equal to the cut width of the boxing strip.

- For the zippered boxing on one long side of the cover, cut two zipper strips, with the length of the strips 1" (2.5 cm) longer than the finished length of the mattress; the cut width of the zipper strips is 1½" (3.8 cm) wider than one-half the finished width of the boxing strip. For the zippered boxing on the short sides of the cover, cut four zipper strips, each 1" (2.5 cm) longer than the finished width of the mattressand 1¼" (3.2 cm) wider than one-half the finished width of the boxing strip.

Tip

Custom-sized zippers are available from upholstery shops and many fabric stores. Or you can use continuous zipper strip, cut it to the right length, and add the zipper tab.

Sewing the futon cover

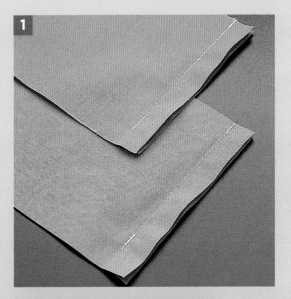

1. Stitch one short zipper strip to each end of one long zipper strip in ½" (1.3 cm) seams, right sides together; start stitching at the raw edge and stop ½" (1.3 cm) from the opposite raw edge. Finish seams, using overlock or zigzag stitch; press open. Repeat, using remaining short and long zipper strips.

2. Place the zipper strips right sides together, matching the raw edges and seams. Machine-baste ¾" (2 cm) from the long edge where stitching of the end seams extends to the raw edge. Finish seams; press open.

3. Fold the strip in half, right sides together, with one seam allowance extending. Place the closed zipper facedown over seam allowances, with the teeth centered on the seam line and the ends of the zipper tape even with the ends of the strip. Machine-baste the zipper tape to the extended seam allowance.

Continued >>

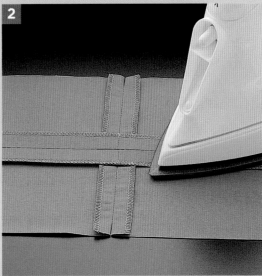

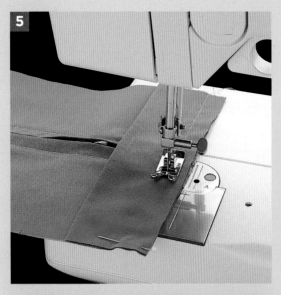

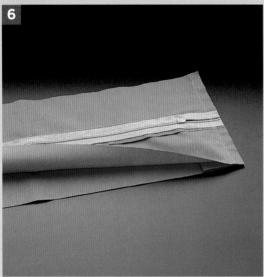

4. Unfold the strip. On right side, center a strip of ³/₄" (2 cm) transparent tape over seam line. Stitch on both sides of the tape, securing the zipper. Remove the tape and basting stitches.

5. Press the zipper tab in half, with wrong sides together. Open the zipper about 2" (5 cm). At the top end of the zipper, place the tab over the zipper strip, right sides up; stitch across the end, a scant ½" (1.3 cm) from the raw edges, stitching carefully over the zipper teeth.

6. Stitch ends of the boxing strip to ends of the zipper strip, right sides together, stitching ½" (1.3 cm) seams; start and stop ½" (1.3 cm) from the raw edges. Finish seams; press open.

7. Pin the boxing strip to the futon cover front, right sides together, matching seams to corners. With the boxing strip faceup, stitch ½" (1.3 cm) seam, pivoting at corners.

8. Pin the opposite side of boxing strip to the futon cover back, right sides together, matching seams to corners; stitch. Finish remaining seams.

9. Open the zipper; turn the futon cover right side out. Insert the futon mattress; close the zipper, hiding the zipper pull under the tab.

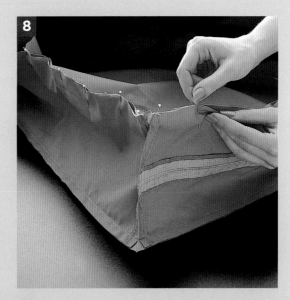

Tip *Working with large pieces of fabric can be awkward. Set up a table next to your sewing cabinet or table, on your left side. By holding excess fabric at the same height as the sewing machine, it will be easier to feed the fabric to the machine and control the extra weight.*

Daybed Cover

A twin bed pushed against a wall provides comfortable, cozy seating for a guest room, dorm room, or studio apartment when you add slipcovered foam bolsters and a fitted mattress cover. Make them as a matched set or use coordinating fabrics, repeating other colors in the room to blend your "new furniture" into the décor.

What you'll need

- Two foam bolster forms
- Polyester upholstery batting
- Decorator fabric
- Cording for welting
- Two zippers the length of the bolsters
- Lining

What you need to know

Fabric stores and specialty foam shops carry precut, four-sided, foam wedge bolsters. They have a wider base than top, with square corners at the back and a slanted front plane. You can make your bolster in one piece or two. Be sure to take measurements of the bed before you buy the foam. The bolster slipcover(s) are made with a zipper centered in the bottom. If you use two bolsters, buy zippers that are almost as long as the bolster sections. If you use one long bolster, buy a continuous zipper or use two upholstery zippers and sew them in with the tops abutting at the center.

This mattress cover has a skirt on all four sides. There are no openings for headboard or footboard posts. If you want to fit your cover on a bed with a headboard and footboard, make separate skirt sections for each side instead of one continuous circle.

Cutting directions

- Measure the circumference and length of the bolster (before wrapping with batting) and add 1" (2.5 cm) to each measurement for seam allowances. Cut fabric to this size, with the lengthwise grain running around the bolster. If you use fabric with large design motifs, cut the fabric so the motifs will be centered on the front of the bolster. Stand the bolster on end and trace the edges on paper. Add ½" (1.3 cm) all around for seam allowances, and cut two end pieces (per bolster), using this pattern.

- Cut fabric for the mattress cover top equal to the size of the mattress plus 1" (2.5 cm) in both directions for seam allowances.

- Measure for the skirt length from the top of the mattress to the floor. Add 2½" (6.5 cm) to this measurement for the cut length of the skirt. Cut four skirt pieces, one for each side, with the widths equal to the cut sides of the mattress top plus 16" (40.5 cm). If possible, railroad the fabric to avoid seams in the front and back. If piecing is necessary, add another ½" (1.3 cm) to each piece for the seam allowance.

- Cut lining pieces the same widths as the skirt pieces and 2" (5 cm) shorter than the skirt pieces.

- Cut bias fabric strips for the welting (page 110), with the length equal to four times (two times if using one bolster) the circumference of the bolster plus the total perimeter of the mattress plus additional length for seaming strips, joining ends, and inconspicuously positioning seams.

Bolster slipcovers

1. Make welting as on page 110. Stitch the welting around the outer edge of the bolster end pieces, following the continuous circle method.

2. Center the zipper alongside one long edge of the large bolster piece and mark the edge at the location of the zipper stops. Pin the long edges, right sides together. Stitch 1/2" (1.3 cm) from the edge, from the side to the first mark; backstitch. Machine-baste to the second mark; backstitch, then finish the seam to the opposite edge.

3. Press the seam allowances open. Center the closed zipper face down over the seam, with the stops at the marks. Glue-baste or pin the zipper tape to the seam allowances only. Finish the seam allowances, catching the zipper tape in the stitches (see photo 3 on page 56).

4. Turn the cover right side out, and spread it flat with the seam facing up. Mark the top and bottom of the zipper coil with pins. Center a strip of 1/2" (1.3 cm) transparent tape over the seam from pin to pin. Topstitch a narrow rectangle along the edges of the tape, using a zipper foot. Stitch slowly as you cross the zipper just beyond the stops. You may need to stitch one side at a time to maneuver the tube of fabric. Remove the tape. Pull threads to the underside and knot. Remove the basting stitches. (See photo 4 on page 56)

5. Make 3/8" (1 cm) clips into the seam allowance on one end of the cover to correspond to the measurements of the sides of the end piece, centering the zipper seam in the bottom section. These clips will mark the corners. Fold the cover crosswise at each location to accurately mark the opposite end.

6. Turn the cover wrong side out. Pin one end piece to one open end of the cover, centering the zipper seam along the bottom edge and aligning clip marks to the corners. The

Continued >>

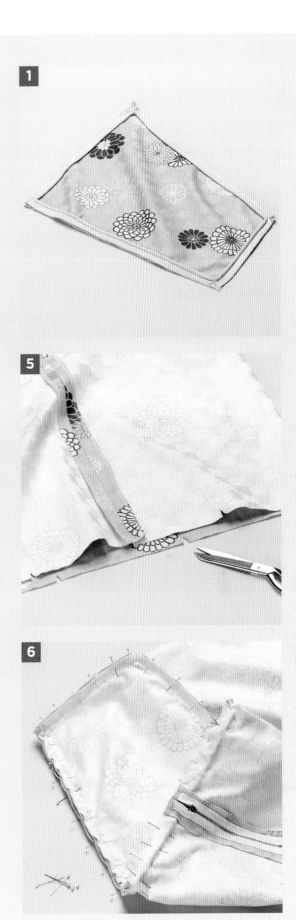

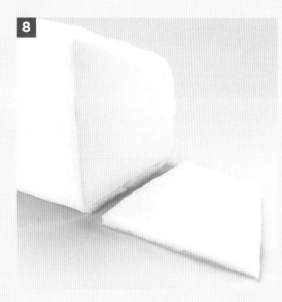

clips will allow the seam allowance to spread apart at the corner. Repeat at the opposite end.

7. Open the zipper partway. Stitch the ends in place, using a zipper foot or welting foot. Turn the cover right side out through the zipper opening.

8. Wrap the foam bolster with polyester upholstery batting, following the directions on page 64. Cut one piece to wrap completely around the top, back, bottom, and front of the bolster. Cut two separate pieces for the ends. Insert the bolster into the cover.

Mattress cover

1. Make welting as on page 110. Stitch the welting around the edge of the mattress cover top, following the continuous circle method.

2. Sew the skirt pieces together in a big circle, using ½" (1.3 cm) seam allowances. Repeat for the lining pieces. Press the seam allowances open.

3. Pin the lower edges of the skirt and lining right sides together, matching seams. Stitch ½" (1.3 cm) from the edges. Press the seam allowances toward the lining.

4. Fold the lining and skirt, wrong sides together, aligning the upper edges. Press. Baste the upper edges together.

5. At the upper edge of the skirt, at each seam, place a pin 1" (2.5 cm) to the left of the seam, a second pin 7" (18 cm) to the right of the seam, and a third pin 15" (38 cm) to the right of the seam. Fold each pleat, bringing the outer pin marks to the center pin mark; pin them in place. The seams will be hidden in the folds of the pleats (see photo 7 on page 34).

6. Check the skirt for fit, and adjust the folds if necessary. Baste across the top of each pleat.

7. Pin the upper edge of the skirt over the welting at the edge of the mattress cover top, right sides together; align the raw edges and match the centers of the pleats to the corners of the top. Clip into the seam allowance at the center of each pleat to allow the fabric to spread and pivot the corner. Stitch, using a welting foot or zipper foot.

8. Press the seam allowances toward the mattress cover top. Arrange the cover over the mattress and smooth in place.

Director's
Chair

●●

Simple slipcovers can be made for inexpensive director's chairs, transforming them into stylish seating. A knife-edge pillow made to fit the seat of the chair adds comfort. Create a pattern for the slipcover by pin-fitting pieces of muslin over the chair frame.

What you'll need

- ⊕ Muslin for making patterns
- ⊕ Decorator fabric or twin-size flat sheet
- ⊕ Polyester upholstery batting and polyester fiberfill

What you need to know

One slipcover and pillow can be made from 3½ yd. (3.2 m) of 54" (137 cm) decorator fabric. Designer sheets can also be used; usually one twin-size sheet is large enough to cut the pieces for one slipcover and pillow.

Cutting directions for the muslin pattern

- Measure the distance from the floor up the back of the chair to the highest point. From the muslin, cut one back piece to the measured distance plus 4" (10 cm); the cut width is equal to the widest part of the chair plus 6" (15 cm).

- Measure the continuous distance from the highest point down the inner back to the seat, from back to front of the seat, then down to the floor. From the muslin, cut one front piece with the cut length equal to the measured distance plus 4" (10 cm); the cut width of the muslin is equal to the widest part of the chair plus 6" (15 cm).

- Measure the continuous distance at the side of the chair from the floor, up and over the arm, then down to the seat. From the muslin, cut one side piece with the cut length equal to the measured distance plus 6" (15 cm); the cut width is equal to the measurement of the chair from the front to the back plus 6" (15 cm).

Pin-fitting the pattern for a director's chair slipcover

1. Pin-mark the center of the chair back and seat. Mark a line lengthwise down the center of the patterns for the back and front seat. Pin the pieces together, ½" (1.3 cm) from the upper edge. Mark the seam line.

2. Pin the fabric to the inner back and seat of the chair, matching centers, with fabric extending onto the floor; position the seam line so it falls between the back edges of the back posts. Smooth fabric over the seat from back to front, allowing slight ease for sitting.

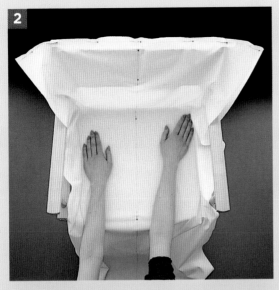

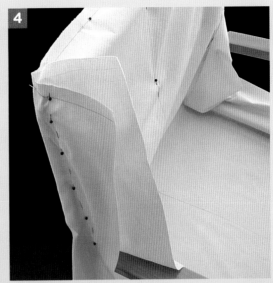

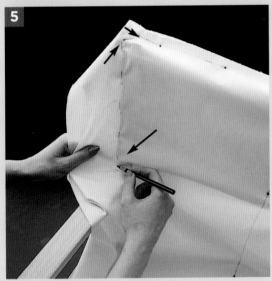

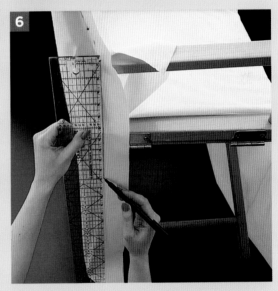

3. Allow back pattern to hang freely to floor. Place excess fabric under back legs of the chair, keeping grain line straight.

4. Wrap back pattern piece around one side of the chair, meeting front pattern piece along the front outer edge of the back post. Pin back to front across the top of the post and along the outer edge of post to arm.

5. Mark dots on both pieces at the back top of post and at point where the post intersects the outer edge of arm (arrows). Mark seam line along pins. Trim excess fabric to within 1" (2.5 cm) of marked seam line.

6. Mark the seam line on the back pattern piece from dot at intersection of post and arm to the floor, using a straightedge; keep the line parallel to the raw edge and perpendicular to the floor.

7. Mark a dot on the front pattern piece at the point where the post intersects the inner edge of the arm. Trim the fabric to within 1" (2.5 cm) of seam line, and clip to dots.

8. Smooth the front pattern piece over the chair seat. Mark seam line along the crease where the seat meets the lower arm. Mark

Continued >>

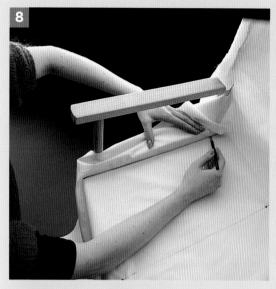

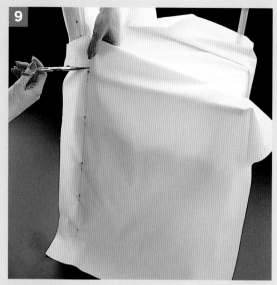

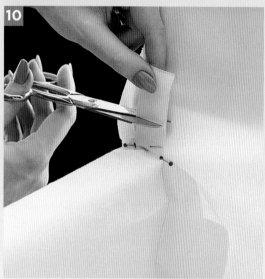

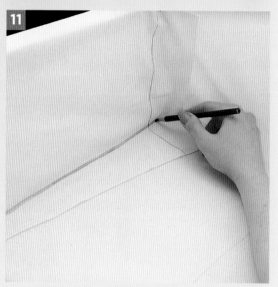

dots on the seam line at the front and back of the seat. Trim excess fabric at the side of seat to within 1" (2.5 cm) of seam line; clip to the front dot.

9. Mark a line on the side pattern piece, 2½" (6.5 cm) from the back edge and parallel to the grain line; pin to seam line of the back pattern, as marked in step 6, allowing about 3" (7.5 cm) to extend onto the floor. Mark a dot at intersection of the outer arm and post; clip to dot. Trim excess fabric to within 1" (2.5 cm) of the seam line, from top of arm to the floor.

10. Wrap the side pattern over the arm and down onto the seat, keeping grain line of the pattern perpendicular to the floor on the outside of the chair. Mark a dot on the side of the pattern at inner arm where it intersects the back post; clip to dot. Pin the side and front pattern pieces together, matching dots. Trim excess fabric to within 1" (2.5 cm) of the seam line between dots.

11. Mark seam line of side pattern along the crease where the seat meets the lower arm. Mark dots on the seam line at the front and back of the seat.

12. Pin the side pattern to the seat of the front pattern along marked seam line, matching the dots. Pin the patterns together from dots at upper arm to dots at the back seat; pins may not follow the previously marked grain line. Mark the seam line. Trim excess fabric to within 1" (2.5 cm) of pinned seam lines. Clip to dots as necessary.

13. Clip to the inner front dot at lower arm. Wrap the inner side pattern piece across the arm front to meet the outer side. Mark the inner and outer front dots at the upper arm, and the outer front dot at the lower arm. Pin together, matching dots; mark the seam line. Trim excess fabric, and clip to dots as necessary.

14. Insert a pin through the matched outer front dots at the lower arm, pinning through to the side of the slipcover. Mark a dot.

15. Pin the side pattern to the front pattern, vertically from dots to the floor. Mark seam line. Pin and mark vertical seam line between dots. Trim to within 1" (2.5 cm) of the marked seam line on the side and front pieces.

Continued >>

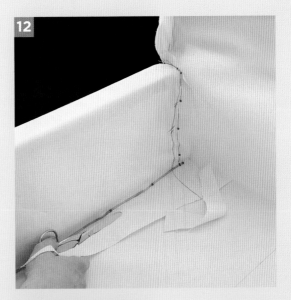

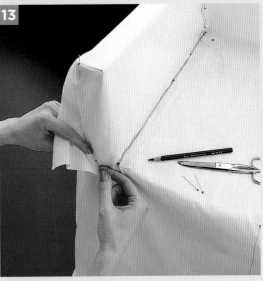

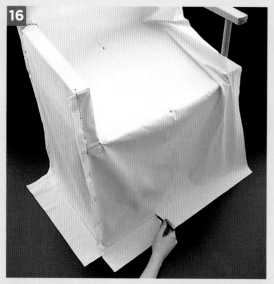

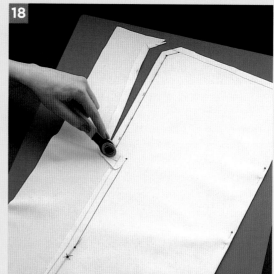

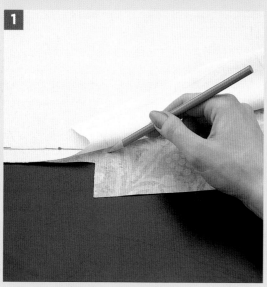

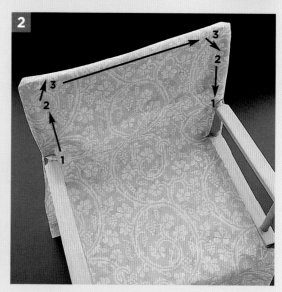

16. Mark the finished length around the lower edge, where patterns reach the floor.

17. Remove the pins that hold the pattern pieces to the chair. Check to see that all seam lines and intersecting dots are marked and match. Remove the pattern from chair. Remove pins from the pattern pieces.

18. Straighten all the seam lines, using a straightedge. Add ½" (1.3 cm) seam allowances to the seams. Add 2" (5 cm) hem allowance to the lower edges. Fold the back and front pattern pieces in half along the center lines. Cut out patterns on the cutting lines.

Sewing the slipcover

1. Lay out and cut the slipcover pieces; turn over the side pattern when cutting the slipcover piece for the opposite side. Transfer all dots from the pattern to slipcover.

2. Pin front and back pieces, right sides together, along the upper edge and back posts, matching dots 1, 2, and 3. Stitch ½" (1.3 cm) seam, starting and ending at dots 1 and pivoting at dots 2 and 3; clip to dots as necessary. Press the seam open; finish the seam. Turn right side out.

3. Pin the side piece to the front piece, matching dots; clip to dots as necessary. Stitch ½" (1.3 cm) seam from dots 4 to 8, as indicated in the photo, pivoting at the corners. Repeat for the opposite side. Press seams open; finish the seams.

4. Pin the front arm of the side piece, right sides together, matching dots 9 and 10 at the upper front arm and dots 11 at the lower arm. Stitch ½" (1.3 cm) seam from dots 9 to 10; pivot at dot 10 and continue stitching through dot 11 to the lower edge of the slipcover. Repeat for the opposite side. Finish the seams and press them open.

5. Stitch ½" (1.3 cm) seam from dot 12 at upper outer arm to the lower edge of the slipcover. Repeat for the opposite side. Press seams open; finish seams.

6. Press under 1" (2.5 cm) twice to wrong side, at lower edge of the slipcover; stitch to make double-fold hem. Place the slipcover on the chair.

7. Cut 1" (2.5 cm) thick polyurethane foam to fit the chair seat. Wrap it with upholstery batting (page 64). Make a knife-edge cushion cover (page 55).

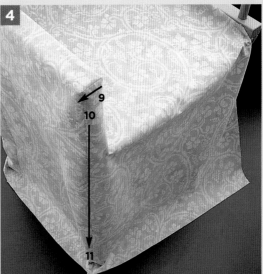

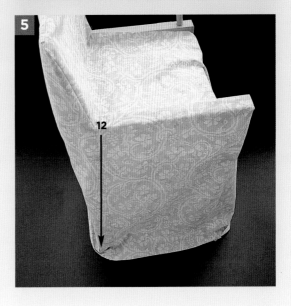

Garden Chair

● ● ○

You can transform a stacking resin chair with a loose-fitting slipcover made of indoor/outdoor decorator fabric. These inexpensive garden chairs come in a variety of shapes and sizes. No one will guess what's under the cover!

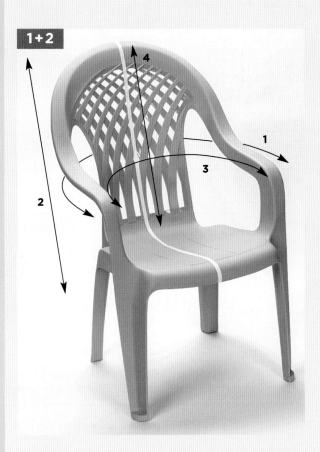

1 + 2

What you'll need

- ⊕ Muslin for making patterns
- ⊕ Indoor/outdoor decorator fabric
- ⊕ Twill tape or grosgrain ribbon

What you need to know

This slipcover consists of four pieces: one piece that wraps around the outside, covering the back and arms; one piece that wraps around the inside, covering the back and arms; one seat piece; and a gathered skirt. The inner and outer pieces are placed with the lengthwise grain running horizontally. They can usually be cut from one width of 54" (137 cm) fabric. To ensure the slipcover fits well, the pattern is pin-fitted with muslin.

Pin-fitting the pattern

1. Mark the center of the chair at the top of the back and at the front and back of the seat with tape. Measure the chair from the front of one arm, around the back, to the front of the other arm (1). Then measure from the top of the back to a few inches below the seat (2). Add 6" (15 cm) in both directions and cut muslin to size. Using a permanent marker, mark a vertical line at the center back and mark the lengthwise grain line of the pattern piece.

2. Measure the inside of the chair from the front of one arm, across the back, to the front of the other arm (3). Then measure from the top of the back to the top of the seat (4). Add 6" (15 cm) in both directions and cut muslin to size. Mark a vertical line at the center back. Mark the lengthwise grain of the pattern piece.

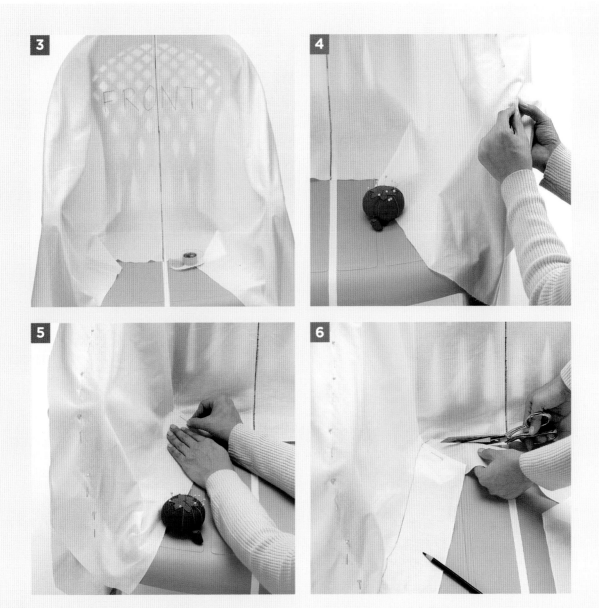

3. Pin the inner and outer patterns together at the center back line. Drape the pinned pattern over the chair, matching the center back lines to the center of the chair. Smooth the inner pattern down over the inner back of the chair, keeping the marked line in the center of the chair. Using double-stick tape, secure the inner pattern to the chair seat at the base of the center line and at the back corners of the seat.

4. Drape the outer pattern around the curve of the chair to the front of the arms, keeping the side grain lines perpendicular to the floor. Pin the inner and outer patterns together along the edge of the chair back

and arms. Trim away some of the excess fabric over the arms to make this step easier. At the front of the arms, pin the patterns together in a straight line to the outer front corner of the seat, rather than fitting it to the shape of the arms. Keep the grain lines perpendicular to the floor.

5. Pin excess fullness of the inner pattern into two pleats at the back corners of the seat so the pattern fits as smoothly as possible.

6. Mark the lower edge of the inner pattern along the outer edge of the seat. Mark a point at each front top corner where the

Continued >>

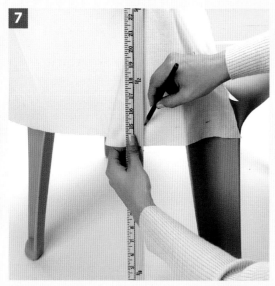

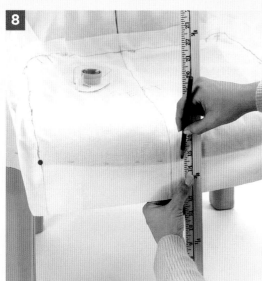

upper and inner covers meet. Trim the pattern to 1" (2.5 cm) beyond the marked line.

7. Measure the distance from the floor to the lower edge of the seat front. Mark a line on the outer pattern the same distance from the floor. Trim the pattern to 1" (2.5 cm) beyond the marked line.

8. Cut muslin a few inches larger than the chair seat, extending down past the lower edge of the seat front. Mark a center line. Secure the pattern to the chair seat with double-stick tape, aligning the centers. Pin the seat piece to the inner back pattern where it aligns to the marked line on the inner pattern. Mark the front of the seat even with the lower edge of the outer pattern. Mark the points where the inner and upper back pieces meet (marked in step 6). Mark the position of the box pleats at the back corners. Trim the seat pattern to 1" (2.5 cm) beyond the marked line.

9. Adjust the fit. Mark all the pinned seam lines and the pleats. Mark points where seams intersect and any other points that will be helpful when stitching the slipcover together.

10. Remove the pattern from the chair. Remove the pins. Cut the pattern pieces 1/2" (1.3 cm) beyond marked seam lines. Fold each piece in half to check for symmetry and adjust the seam lines if necessary. Use the pattern pieces to cut out the decorator fabric. Transfer all marks. For the slipcover skirt, measure from the lower edge of the seat front (same measurement taken in step 7) and add 2 1/2" (6.5 cm) for seam and hem allowances. Cut two strips equal to this measurement across the width of the decorator fabric and trim the *selvages*.

Sewing the slipcover

1. Staystitch the lower edge of the inner back piece a scant ½" (1.3 cm) from the edge. Fold the pleats at the marks and baste in place. Pin the upper edges of the inner and outer back pieces, right sides together, matching marks. Stitch a ½" (1.3 cm) seam.

2. Pin the seat to the lower edge of the inner back, right sides together, aligning the pleats to the marks at the back corners. Clip the seam allowance of the inner back as necessary to allow it to fit around the curves of the seat. The lower front edge of the seat will align to the lower edge of the outer slip-cover. Stitch.

3. Sew the short ends of the skirt strips right sides together and press the seams open. Finish one long edge with serging or zigzag stitches. Press under 1½" (3.8 cm) and top-stitch the hem in place.

4. Pin-mark the raw edge of the skirt in fourths. Between each set of pin marks, stitch two rows of gathering threads. Also pin-mark the lower edge of the slipcover in fourths.

5. Pin the skirt to the slipcover, right sides together, matching pin marks. Pull each set of gathering threads to evenly gather the skirt to fit the cover; knot the thread ends to secure. Stitch the skirt in place and press.

6. Cut two 24" (61 cm) lengths of twill tape or ribbon. Fold the strips in half and stitch one securely to the seam allowances on the underside of the slipcover at each seat back corner.

7. Put the slipcover on the chair. Lift the skirt and tie the twill-tape ties to the back chair legs to hold the slipcover in place.

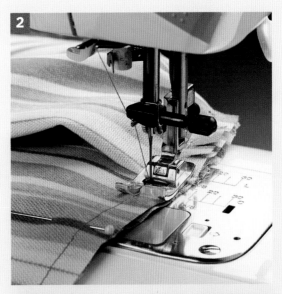

Outdoor Chaise

●●

Custom-fitted cushions will make your chairs and chaise lounges comfortable and stylish. These soft cushions are filled with layers of polyester upholstery batting and covered with the indoor/outdoor fabric of your choice.

The cushions are sewn with a simple mock-box construction that requires only front and back pieces (no separate sides). Stitching lines across the cushions allow them to bend and conform to the shape of the furniture. Stitching lines can also be used to create a head or leg rest.

What you'll need

- ⊕ Indoor/outdoor decorator fabric
- ⊕ Polyester upholstery batting
- ⊕ Aerosol adhesive for polyurethane foam

What you need to know

Depending on the style of furniture, cushions can be secured with ties or a hood. Plan ahead before you start the project. Ties can be secured around the frame of many metal and wooden furniture pieces and are sometimes inserted through the openwork of a mesh deck or between straps, bars, or slats. For a cushion that is reversible, stitch the ties at the side seams. If the furniture does not have any open areas for ties, create a hood to fit over the back. How-to steps for a hood or ties follow later in the project.

Cushions with Rounded Corners

1. Measure the width of the chair or chaise frame from side to side (1). Measure the distance from the top of the frame to the desired depth of the headrest (2). Measure the length of the chair or chaise lounge frame from the top of the back to the front of the frame (3). Measure the distance from the front edge to the back of the seat (4); if the chaise lounge has a curved or bent legrest area, also measure the depth of the leg rest from the front edge to the highest point on the frame (5). Record the measurements.

2. Add 4" (10 cm) to the length and width to allow for seam allowances and the thickness of the cushion. In addition, add 2" (5 cm) to the length for each stitching line across the cushion. Cut two pieces of fabric to this size.

3. Trace the upper and lower curved corners of the frame on paper. Trim the paper along the curved lines.

4. Place the pattern for the curves at the corners of the layered fabric, with the marked lines tapering to the raw edges at the top and sides; pin in place. Trim the fabric along the curves.

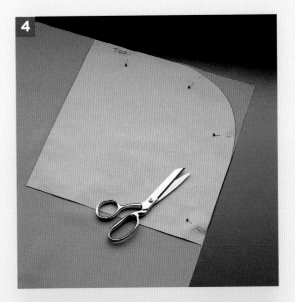

5. Measure from the upper edge of the fabric a distance equal to the desired depth of the headrest plus 3" (7.5 cm). Using chalk, mark a line on the right side of each piece across the width. Mark the ends of the lines on the wrong sides.

6. For a chair or chaise with a leg extension, measure from the lower edge of the fabric a distance equal to the measurement from the front of the frame to the back of the seat plus 3" (7.5 cm). Using chalk, mark a line across the right side of each piece. Mark the ends of the lines on the wrong sides of the fabric pieces (photo below, right).

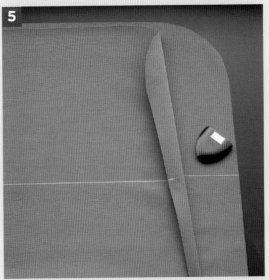

6. For a chaise lounge with a bent leg rest, measure from the lower edge of the fabric a distance equal to the depth of the leg rest plus 3" (7.5 cm); mark a chalk line on the right side of each piece across the width. Also measure from the lower edge of the fabric a distance equal to the measurement from the front of the frame to the back of the seat plus 5" (12.7 cm); mark a chalk line on the right side of each fabric piece. Mark the ends of both lines on the wrong sides of the pieces (photo on page 104).

7. Cut and attach the hood piece, if desired (page 106). Place the front and back cushion pieces right sides together; pin, matching the marks on the sides.

8. Machine-stitch ½" (1.3 cm) from the raw edges, starting on one long side, just beyond the rounded corner; stitch across the end, down the opposite long side, across the opposite end, and stop just beyond the last corner.

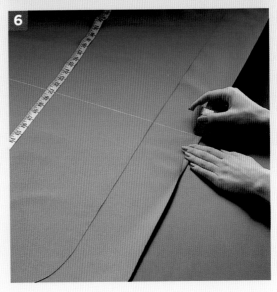

Continued >>

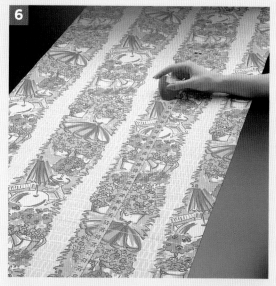

9. Stitch ½" (1.3 cm) from the raw edges on the remaining long side, starting and stopping 2" (5 cm) from each marked line; this leaves an opening in each section of the cushion. Clip the seam allowances of the rounded corners.

10. Turn the cover right side out through one opening. Make and position the ties, if desired (page 107). On the sides of the cushion, fold 1" (2.5 cm) inverted tucks at the stitching lines as shown and pin in place; enclose the ties, if any, in the tucks. Pin the front and back cushion pieces together along the stitching lines.

11. Stitch along the marked stitching lines, stitching the tucks in place at the sides. If the cushion has ties, catch the ties in the stitching of the tucks.

12. Cut four pieces of polyester upholstery batting for the area at the top of the cushion, cutting the pieces 1" (2.5 cm) wider than the chair or chaise lounge frame and 1" (2.5 cm) longer than the depth of the headrest; round the corners. Stack and secure two pieces of batting together, applying aerosol adhesive to both inner sides. Repeat to secure all four layers.

13. Repeat step 12 for the section at the bottom of the cushion, using four pieces of batting 1" (2.5 cm) wider than the frame and 1" (2.5 cm) longer than the measurement from the front of the frame to the back of the seat. If you're making a cushion for a chaise lounge with a leg rest, use pieces 1" (2.5 cm) longer than the depth of the leg rest.

14. Repeat step 12 for the middle section or sections of the cushion, using pieces of batting 1" (2.5 cm) wider than the frame, with the length of each piece equal to the distance between the stitching lines minus 1" (2.5 cm).

15. Fold the layered batting for the headrest in half crosswise; insert it into the headrest area through the opening, pulling the batting all the way to the opposite side of the

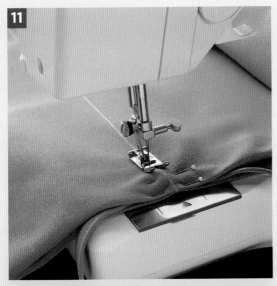

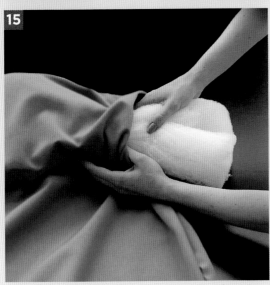

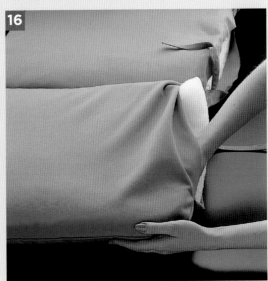

cushion. Unfold the batting and smooth it in place. Adjust the position of the batting as needed, filling the corners with pieces of batting, if necessary.

16. Repeat step 15 for the remaining areas of the cushion, using corresponding sections of the batting.

17. Pin the openings on the side of the cushion closed; slipstitch.

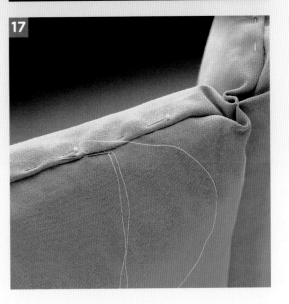

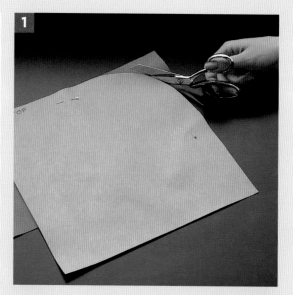

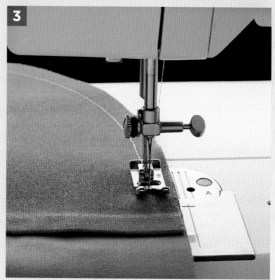

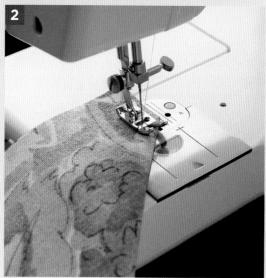

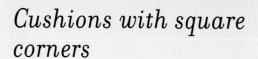

Cushions with square corners

1. Measure the chair or chaise frame and cut the fabric as on page 102, steps 1 and 2. At the corners, use chalk to mark a 1½" (3.8 cm) square; cut on the marked lines.

2. Fold the corners, matching the raw edges; stitch a ½" (1.3 cm) seam, 2" (5 cm) long, as shown. Complete the cushion as on pages 103 to 105, steps 5 to 17; in step 7, fold the corner seam allowances of the front and back pieces in opposite directions to distribute the bulk.

Hooded back

1. Cut the fabric for the hood piece, 4" (10 cm) wider than the chair or lounge frame and 8½" (21.8 cm) long. For a cushion with rounded corners, trim the upper corners of the hood, using the pattern from step 3 on page 102 for cushions with rounded corners.

2. On the lower edge of the hood piece, make a ½" (1.3 cm) double-fold hem.

3. Pin the hood to the cushion back, right sides up; baste near the edges. Complete the cushion as on pages 103 to 105, steps 7 to 17.

Ties

1. Cut four 2" x 24" (5 x 61 cm) strips of fabric for the ties. Press them in half lengthwise, wrong sides together; unfold. Fold the raw edges to the center; press.

2. Refold the ties in half, enclosing the raw edges. Edgestitch close to both long edges of the ties.

3. Pin the ties to the sides of the cushion at the marked stitching lines for the headrest and back of the seat. Complete the cushion as in steps 10 to 17 for cushions with rounded corners.

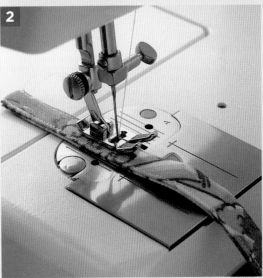

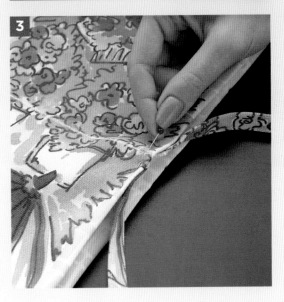

Tip

Instead of layering polyester upholstery batting, you can cut pieces of indoor/outdoor cushion insert material, such as NU-Foam® by Fairfield. This polyester product acts like foam but is treated to resist mildew and it will not disintegrate or lose it's shape.

Slipcover Basics

Whether you are making simple dining chair covers or a more complicated fitted slipcover for a sofa, there are some basic techniques you'll use over and over. Follow these guidelines for successful results.

Laying out and cutting the fabric

Whenever possible, lay out all the pattern pieces on the fabric before you start to cut. This allows you to rearrange the pieces as necessary to make the best use of the fabric.

When a patterned fabric with an all-over design is used for slipcovers, little matching is required. When seaming widths of fabric together, such as for a sofa, the pattern should be matched. Patterned fabrics can also be matched at the seam line on the upper edge of the skirt, if desired, following the technique for boxed cushions (page 62). If a patterned fabric with a one-way design is used, be careful to lay the pieces in the correct direction of the fabric.

Center large motifs in a print fabric on the top and bottom of the cushion. For best results, also align the design so it continues down the back of the furniture, onto the cushion, and down the skirt.

Tips for laying out and cutting the slipcover fabric

- Center large motifs, such as floral clusters, on the back, sides, cushions, and on the top of the arms.

- Center the prominent stripe of a striped fabric on the center placement line of the outside and inside back pieces and on the cushion pieces. Decide which direction the stripes will run on the arms; usually it looks best to have the stripes run in the same direction as the stripes on the skirt.

- Cut the skirt pieces for a self-lined skirt, placing the fold line at the lower edge of the skirt on a crosswise fold of the fabric. Self-lined skirts hang better than single-layer skirts with a hem.

- Cut arm pieces, right sides together, using the first piece as the pattern for cutting the second piece.

- Mark names of pieces on the wrong side of the fabric, using chalk. Abbreviations like "D" for deck, "IB" for inside back, and "OA" for outside arm work well.

- Transfer all markings, including notches and dots, from the muslin pieces to the slipcover fabric.

How to match a patterned fabric

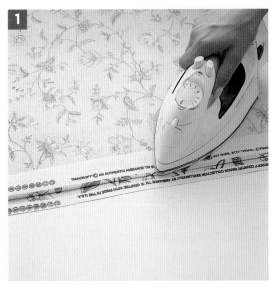

1. Position fabric widths, right sides together, matching selvages. Fold back the upper selvage until the pattern matches; lightly press fold line.

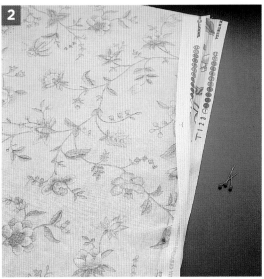

2. Unfold the selvage; pin fabric widths together on the fold line. Check match from the right side.

3. Repin the fabric widths so pins are perpendicular to the fold line; stitch on the fold line, using a straight stitch. Trim fabric to finished length.

Tip

How much fabric do you need? Generally, a chair requires about 7 to 8 yd. (6.4 to 7.35 m) of fabric; a love seat, 10 to 12 yd. (9.15 to 11.04 m); and a sofa, 16 to 20 yd. (14.72 to 18.4 m). These amounts include matching welting and a skirt with pleats at the corners. Allow additional fabric for cushions and ruffled or box-pleated skirts. Each cushion requires 1 to 1½ yd. (0.92 to 1.4 m) of fabric. For a ruffled or box-pleated skirt, allow 1 yd. (.092 m) extra for a chair, 2 to 3 yd. (1.85 to 2.75 m) for a love seat, and 4 yd. (3.7 m) for a sofa.

Cording with a diameter of $5/32"$ (3.8 mm) is the usual cording for cushions and slipcover seams. Cut the fabric strips $1\frac{1}{2}"$ (3.8 cm) wide. Cording with a diameter of $\frac{1}{4}"$ (6 mm) is slightly larger for similar applications. Cut the fabric strips $1\frac{3}{4}"$ (4.5 cm) wide. To determine how wide to cut the fabric strips on other sizes of cording, wrap a piece of fabric or paper around the cording. Pin it together, encasing the cording. Cut $\frac{1}{2}"$ (1.3 cm) from the pin. Measure the width, and cut strips to match.

The instructions below show you how to attach welting in a continuous circle, such as for a boxed cushion. When a welted seam will be intersected by another seam, remove $\frac{1}{2}"$ (1.3 cm) of the cording from the end of the welting to prevent bulk at the seam line.

Decorative welting

Just as piping is used in garments to outline a fashion detail, welting is used in home décor sewing to define and support seams. Welting is fabric-covered cording, sewn into a seam to provide extra strength and a decorative finishing touch.

Fabric strips for welting can be cut on the bias or the straight grain. Straight-grain welting requires less fabric but is only suitable for seams that are straight because it is less flexible. Use bias fabric strips for welting that will be sewn around curves. Bias welting strips do not have to be cut on the true bias. Cutting the strips at an angle less than 45 degrees gives the flexibility of bias grain but requires less yardage. For stripes and plaids, bias welting does not require matching.

Making and attaching welting (continuous)

1. Center the cording on the wrong side of the strip. Fold the strip over the cording, aligning the raw edges. Using a zipper foot, machine-baste close to the cording.

2. Attach the welting to the right side of the slipcover piece with raw edges aligned. Begin stitching 2" (5 cm) from the end of the welting; stitch on the basting line. To ease at rounded corners, clip into the seam allowances up to the basting. To prevent welted seams from puckering, take care not to stretch either welting or fabric as the seam is stitched.

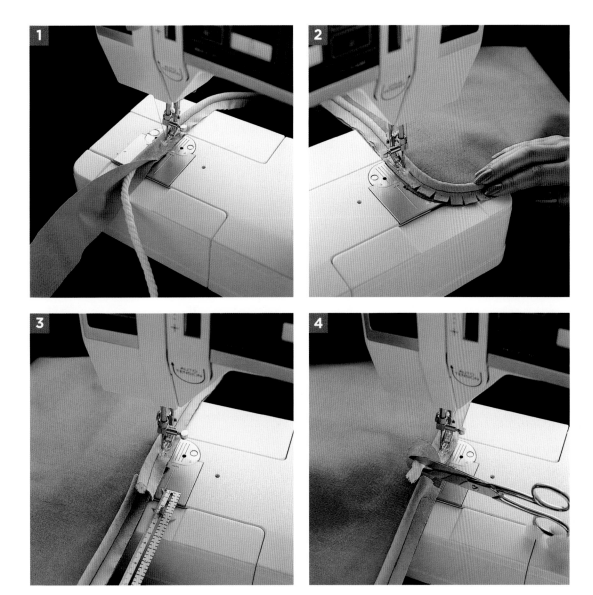

3. Stop stitching 2" (5 cm) from the point where the cording ends will meet. Leaving the needle in the fabric, cut off one end so it overlaps the other end by 1" (2.5 cm).

4. Remove 1" (2.5 cm) of stitching from each end of the welting. Trim the cording ends so they just meet.

5. Fold under ½" (1.3 cm) of the overlapping fabric. Lap it around the other end; finish stitching.

Terms to Know

Bias. Any diagonal line intersecting the lengthwise and crosswise grains of fabric. While woven fabric is very stable on the lengthwise and crosswise grains, it has considerable stretch on the bias.

Crosswise grain. On woven fabrics, the crosswise grain is perpendicular to the selvages. Fabric has slight "give" in the crosswise grain.

Cut length. The total length at which fabric pieces should be cut for the slipcover. It includes allowances for any hems or seams.

Cut width. The total width the fabric should be cut. If more than one width of fabric is needed, the cut width refers to the entire panel after seams are sewn.

Darts. Fabric is folded and stitched to remove excess fullness and give shape to an item. For instance, darts are sewn at the front corners of a chair seat cover to make the fabric conform to the front corners of the seat.

Directional print. The design printed on the fabric may have definite up and down directions, such as flowers growing upward. All pieces of a slipcover should be cut so that the print will run in the correct direction when you are finished.

Finish. To improve the durability of a seam, the raw edges are secured with stitches that prevent them from fraying. This can be done with zigzag stitches that wrap over the edge or with serging.

Lengthwise grain. On woven fabrics, the lengthwise grain runs parallel to the selvages. Fabrics are generally stronger along the lengthwise grain.

Lining. A fabric backing sewn to the face fabric to provide extra body.

Muslin. This medium-weight, plainly woven cotton fabric is relatively inexpensive, so it is often used for drafting patterns when paper isn't feasible.

Pattern repeat. The lengthwise distance from one distinctive point in the fabric pattern, such as the tip of a particular petal in a floral pattern, to the same point in the next pattern design.

Railroading. Normally the lengthwise grain of the fabric runs vertically in a slipcover. Since decorator fabric is usually 54" (137 cm) wide, slipcover pieces that are wider than this, such as skirts, must have vertical seams joining additional widths of fabric. Railroading means the fabric is turned sideways, so the lengthwise grain runs horizontally. The full width can then be cut in one piece, eliminating the need for any seams.

Self-lined. A fabric panel lined to the edge with the same fabric. Rather than cutting two pieces and sewing them together, one double-length piece is cut, folded right sides together, and stitched on the remaining three sides, so the lower edge will have a fold instead of a seam or hem.

Selvage. The narrow, tightly woven edges of the fabric that do not ravel or fray. These should be cut away on firmly woven fabrics before seaming to prevent puckering of seams.